ALSO BY KAY ALLENBAUGH

Chocolate for a Woman's Soul

Chocolate for a Woman's Heart

Chocolate for a Lover's Heart

Chocolate for a Mother's Heart

Chocolate for a Woman's Spirit

Chocolate for a Teen's Soul

Chocolate for a Woman's Blessings

Chocolate for a Teen's Heart

Chocolate for a Woman's Dreams

Chocolate for a Teen's Spirit

77 Stories that Honor

Your Strength

and Wisdom

A FIRESIDE BOOK
Published by Simon & Schuster
New York   London   Toronto   Sydney   Singapore

CHOCOLATE

for a

WOMAN'S
COURAGE

KAY ALLENBAUGH

FIRESIDE
Rockefeller Center
1230 Avenue of the Americas
New York, NY 10020

FIRESIDE and colophon are registered trademarks
of Simon & Schuster, Inc.

For information regarding special discounts for bulk purchases,
please contact Simon & Schuster Special Sales:
1-800-456-6798 or business@simonandschuster.com

Manufactured in the United States of America

1   3   5   7   9   10   8   6   4   2

Library of Congress Cataloging-in-Publication Data
Chocolate for a woman's courage / [compiled by] Kay Allenbaugh.
p.   cm.
"A Fireside book."
1. Women—United States—Anecdotes.   2. Courage—Anecdotes.
3. Wisdom—Anecdotes.
I. Allenbaugh, Kay.
HQ1421 .C494 2002
305.4'0973—dc21   2002075831

ISBN 0-7432-3699-8 (pbk.)

This book is dedicated

to women who personify courage

and to the ones yet to step forward.

May your lives be doubly blessed.

CONTENTS

III

LASTING LEGACIES

IV

ANIMAL HOUSE

V

KNOWING WHAT'S BEST

VI

A LOVING TOUCH

VII

A POSITIVE POWER SURGE

VIII

FAMILY MATTERS

IX

ALL THINGS DIVINE

INTRODUCTION

We have been hearing so much about acts of courage during the last year. Many of these were acts of heroism that will burn in our hearts forever. And many others were the quieter, more mundane acts of waiting, helping, and finding ways to move forward with our lives.

Chocolate for a Woman's Courage celebrates this quieter kind of unsung bravery that women across the country embody every single day. These seventy-seven touching, true stories will remind you of the ways in which we can be willing to take risks, stand up for family and friends, claim our true spirit, face a life-threatening illness, laugh at our own foibles, and celebrate someone else's success.

Courage is nothing new to women—just ask your mother! As the contributors to *Chocolate for a Woman's Courage* share, some of the bravest things they have done have meant finding inner strength—the strength to dig deep within yourself to take that next important step in your career, even though you are afraid, or to survive the loss of a loved one and create a new life, or to raise wonderful children in spite of all the times you second guessed yourself, or faithfully to listen to that small, still voice that guides you daily. These stories will inspire you to remember all the ways that you've been courageous so far, and encourage you to move forward with what is yet to come.

Ironically, it's often the seemingly small things in life that simply require us to "show up" that can create the most stress. That can mean saying no when it's necessary, trusting your intuition, being brave enough to forgive rather than harbor ill will, or using your God-given talents in a beautiful way. But whatever your challenge you will find sweet resolve in these pages. Hope and renewed determination shine through them. You will find yourself identifying with the Chocolate sisters who have faced circumstances much like the ones you face yourself—both little and big—ultimately triumphing as they discover what they value most.

As you curl up with *Chocolate for a Woman's Courage*, I have a wish for you. May you take a journey from your head to your heart, receive the loving touch that is offered, gather more wisdom to use in your own life, and listen for the Divine messages coming your way as you let these stories settle into your soul.

I
THE JOURNEY
FROM
HEAD TO HEART

Courage is like a muscle; we strengthen it with use.

RUTH GORDON

A SPIRIT-FILLED WALK

*F*or years now, I have made it my practice to walk several times a week, or daily if the weather is good. I have found the habit of walking to be extremely valuable in physical, spiritual, and emotional ways. My favorite place to walk near my home is a graveyard that has a paved area around the lush grounds, making for comfortable walking in peaceful surroundings.

One day I had been walking for about five miles. The weather outside had gotten hotter, and I must have looked like a sight to behold. I pushed myself at a faster and faster pace, and my shorts and T-shirt were damp with perspiration, and my hair clung to my face, wet and sweaty.

As I rounded one corner, I saw a gold minivan approaching that I had seen many times before. The woman inside was middle-aged and always had a little dog on her lap. Because she wore dark sunglasses whenever I saw her, I could never have identified her had I seen her elsewhere in the community. However, I recognized her at the graveyard because it was always the same van, the same dog, and her actions were always the same. She would roll down her window, perch the dog on her lap—with its neck craning out the window—and they both would stare at the graves for what seemed like forever, while she cried. I always wondered what her story was, but had never talked to her before.

As I rounded the bend, I heard a voice whisper, "Go and ask her if you can pray for her, to be healed." I am a pastor, but neither this woman nor anyone else probably would have recognized me as such at the time. Sticky, grimy, and smelly, I thought, *This woman would think I'm crazy. And perhaps I am crazy! What if this is just "me" talking to myself?* So I prayed, "God, I don't know if this is really you or if it's just me. If you really want me to talk to her, let her still be there as I round the corner the next time."

On my final lap, she was still there. I felt strongly that I should obey the prompting of what I now felt certain was God.

I approached her van and quietly said, "Ma'am, I know I look like a scary sight right now, and I ask you to excuse my appearance—but I felt directed to stop and talk to you. I have seen you here on different occasions, and I don't know who you lost, but I know they must be really important to you. As I was walking, God told me to stop and ask you if I could pray for you, for healing."

At that, she sobbed pretty much uncontrollably. Mysteriously, I was prepared in a practical way for her tears. Before I had left on my walk that day, I had the indescribable urge to fill my pockets with about ten tissues, something I have never done before in years of walking. As she cried, I just stood there pulling the Kleenex out of my pockets and comforting her. Between sobs, she choked out, "I've been praying, 'Oh God, if you really care about me, send someone, just ONE PERSON to tell me—and to care.' " At that point I was crying, too, and we shared the tissues.

Once she was able to speak more easily, she told me that her husband, Jack, had died an early death from cancer. They had been together since they were teenagers and were always deeply in love right up until the day he died. His death was so sudden, so unfair. They were never able to have children, but the little dog was a very real part of the family. She went on to tell me how much their animal still missed Jack as well. She spoke of just wanting "one more chance to hold Jack . . . one more chance to love him."

Oh, how her heart ached for her Jack. Since his death the previous year, she had stopped all the activities that had kept her busy. Except for sitting in the house and crying, the highlight of her day was making trips to the graveyard. A year after Jack's death, her healing had not even begun. The pain was still oozing out on a daily basis.

When she was finished sharing her story with me, I had the privilege of joining hands with her and praying a prayer of healing for her. Her face broke out into a smile and through the tears she said, "Thank you, I really do feel different." I apologized for my appearance, again, and she said, "Don't apologize, you're beautiful!" Knowing how I looked, I'm convinced she was talking about beauty on the inside.

The next day I came back to the graveyard to walk. I was secretly hoping not to see my new friend in the minivan. I was hoping beyond hope that through our prayer the day before, perhaps, she had experienced some relief and didn't feel the pressing need to make her daily trip to the graveyard.

My heart soon sank, as I saw the van rounding the corner. But as she got closer, I squinted my eyes to see . . . something new. No sunglasses!

As she brought the van to a halt, she stuck her head out the window with a huge smile and said, "Well, hello there, friend!"

Pleasantly surprised, I said, "Hi! How are you today? I mean how are you, *really?* Did yesterday help at all?"

"Yes, that's why I'm here," she replied. "I have called nearly everybody I know in these last twenty-four hours to tell them that God sent me a special angel yesterday to deliver a message to me personally. I *know* He really cares! And I wanted to come up here and tell Jack that I still love him as much as ever, but perhaps there won't be the need for me to visit daily anymore. It's time to begin healing. I'm moving forward!"

What a joy it was to see hope for the future brought into this woman's life and her eyes sparkling with renewed joy.

Although I had never met Jack personally, in a very real sense it feels like I know him. His wife has often described in detail how wonderful he was, and the love and passion they shared right up until his death. I often find myself thinking about how I wish everyone I knew experienced an earthly love relationship like this, one that is stronger than death. And for those of us who have, may we appreciate it in the fullest sense, realizing that life indeed is short. May we love deeply, passionately, and unreservedly.

I have continued my walks in the graveyard, and I periodically see her, though the times are few and far between. Meeting is a treasure. We have never kept in touch other than in the graveyard. But each time we meet, we part with a hug and an "I love you"— both of us more assured than ever that we never walk alone.

DEANNA DOSS SHRODES

Having a baby is definitely a labor of love.
JOAN RIVERS

RISING TO THE OCCASION

I *went into labor five weeks before my first child was due.* My contractions started off four minutes apart, and my doctor told me to go straight to the hospital. When I arrived, I found out I was three centimeters dilated.

"We're going to give you some shots to try to stop your labor," a nurse told me. At that point, I didn't care what they did—I just wanted the pain to go away.

I spent the night in the hospital, and by the next morning, my contractions had stopped. I was sent home with pills to prevent more contractions and orders for complete bed rest.

When the pain started again that afternoon, I begged my doctor to let me deliver. "I can't do this anymore!" I cried. "Just get the kid out and make it stop hurting!"

My doctor patiently explained that if my baby was born five weeks early, she could be fine. Or she could have immature respiratory and digestive systems, and need lots of medical care. Since I hadn't dilated any more, he strongly recommended trying to postpone delivery again, to give the baby more time to develop. I grudgingly agreed and was taken back to the same hospital room I had vacated only hours earlier.

A little while later, my husband went downstairs to complete my admissions paperwork. When he returned, he told me that he had met another father-to-be from our childbirth class, whose wife (also named Carol) was being admitted.

The other Carol had been having painless contractions for hours. By the time she realized what was happening and got to the hospital, she was eight centimeters dilated—too far along to stop labor. They were expecting their baby at any time.

That's not fair, I thought. She has painless contractions and gets to have her baby now. And here I am being stuck with one needle after another to try to postpone my labor—which isn't the painless kind. While the medicine worked to stop my contractions, I lay on my hospital bed and sulked.

When my pain finally went away, I started thinking about Carol. Her due date was a week later than mine was, so her baby would be six weeks early. I had spent two days hearing about the potential medical problems my baby could face if my labor wasn't stopped. Now Carol was in labor and her baby might actually face those problems. I started praying for this woman I barely knew and her baby. "Please, God, let this baby be healthy," I pleaded. "Please let everything be okay."

While I was wishing for Carol to have a healthy baby, I felt a little foot (or maybe it was an elbow or a fist) jabbing me—hard— from the inside. Instinctively, I reached down to caress the little limb, and I realized that someone else was involved in all this, too. Up until that moment, I had seen my pregnancy as being all about me—my nausea, my leg cramps, my sciatic pain, my premature labor—and never about the baby growing inside me.

"I guess this hasn't been much fun for you, either," I said as I rubbed my belly. "And it could be even worse for you if you're born too early. So you just stay in there and grow for a few more weeks like the doctor said, so you'll be strong and healthy."

Once again, my labor was stopped, and the next morning I was discharged. On our way out, my husband and I stopped at the nursery, where Carol's baby was being observed. Tears filled my eyes as I looked through the glass at her beautiful boy. "Is he okay?" I asked the nurse.

"Oh, yes," she told me, "he's perfect."

Thankful that he was healthy, I blew him a kiss and then wrapped my arms around my abdomen, giving my own baby a hug. Then I left the hospital—still pregnant, but feeling like a mother for the very first time.

CAROL SJOSTROM MILLER

I DREAM OF SHAWNA

*I*t is Thursday evening, just before a long weekend, and instead of relaxing before an extra day of recreation, our family is making frantic preparations: cleaning dark corners, decorating, and buying delicacies. Anticipation is high as we prepare for the arrival of the love of my sixteen-year-old son's computer-focused life, his cyber-girlfriend, Shawna.

It is hard for me to believe. Our Jake, a gawky, scrawny, six-foot-tall mass of bone and sinew with few social graces and fewer words, has somehow not only electronically entranced a female of the species, but convinced her and her father to drive the six hundred miles up the coast to meet us all in person. Usually cool, Jake is a little nervous even though he claims to know Shawna well from five months of chatting on the Internet. They have exchanged pictures, via snail mail, and hers are on display by the computer terminal. She is an attractive girl with dark hair and a snazzy personality that shows even in the Polaroid. It is easy to imagine that he would want to impress her.

The evening wears on. After pacing miles between the kitchen and living room, Jake cleans his room (unasked), burning a scented candle and inviting me in to see if everything smells okay. Smell must be on his mind. He has showered, washed all his bed linens and clothes, brushed and flossed his teeth twice, and sent me to the store for new, better-smelling mouthwash.

"Jacob," I finally say, "what's up?"

"Mom," he replies, "I don't want to smell like a boy!"

Late that night it feels like Christmas Eve. I am exhausted from a day full of activity and anticipation. The house gleams, the laundry is folded and put away, floors are clean and polished, the smell of freshly baked cookies lingers in the shiny kitchen. I collapse on the couch as Jake rises.

"I'm going to bed," he says.

"So early? It's only nine o'clock," I say.

He gives me one of his sardonic looks and stalks off. Minutes later I hear the shower.

As I relax into the couch I am aware of a feeling that's been nagging at the edge of my mind all day. I am worried. Worried that this girl, about whom we really know nothing, will break my son's heart. That she'll take one look at him and decide it was all a mistake. Or worse, she'll mesmerize him and become the only influence in his young, inexperienced life. He'll become her love slave, unwilling and unable to listen to himself or to anyone else. Me, for instance. I stop myself in midfantasy, knowing that if I continue to spin out this tale it will become increasingly depressing.

As I think about it, I am shocked to realize that I've been walking a fine line between jealousy and lack of faith. Jealousy of their youth, their passion, and lack of faith in my son's ability to sustain a relationship. I don't know which disturbs me more. It is a thankless task, this being a parent. It's so much work, and just when you think you can see an end to it, it turns on you, and the mirror of yourself in your children becomes too evident to ignore. I see myself in the fledgling relationship of my son and this girl, this Shawna, as a controlling, meddling, overbearing mother. "But I just want him to be happy," I inwardly wail as my mind answers, "Yeah, right. As long as you can control everything."

I am too tired to indulge in this kind of revealing self-therapy, and soon I, too, am in bed, knowing that all too soon the new day will arrive and, with it, Shawna and her father. I sleep fitfully, awakening several times during the night, marveling at my state of anxiety. If *I'm* this jittery, how must Jake be feeling?

Toward morning, I fall into a deep sleep and begin to dream. In my dream Shawna has arrived and is standing by the door. This Shawna is not like any of her pictures. She is tall and ungraceful, uneasily clutching at her elbows. Her dull, brown hair stands up in strange clumps, and she wears thick, horn-rimmed glasses. Her eyes look suspiciously like they might cross at any moment. I reach out to give her a hug, and she shrinks from me ungraciously. I am impatient and sorry for her at the same time. Then Jake comes into the room with a new girlfriend, a girl who looks suspiciously like a smaller version of himself: red curly hair, freckles, lively, cute. In my dream I know her; she is his childhood friend, his sidekick. I am shocked that they have so suddenly become a couple when the day before they were just friends. But suddenly, faced with Shawna, he has realized that his real, true love is the red-haired buddy.

The dream ends with the four us in that room: Shawna, eyes glued to the floor; Jacob and his dream buddy standing close together, smiling, ignoring everyone else; and me in the middle, happy for Jacob, but wondering what we are going to do about Shawna.

I awake, wondering at the intensity of the dream, knowing it's important. Later, I am at the kitchen sink, my hands in warm, soapy water, when it hits me. I think of how the dream Shawna resembles Jake: his fumbling, adolescent, uncomfortable self. Before I even finish the thought, I realize that the red-haired dream girlfriend also resembles him. She is smart, good-natured, humorous, and ready to love and be loved. For some reason I begin to weep, and I stand at the sink for some minutes, tears running down my face.

The rest of the morning is spent on last-minute details: polishing the already clean kitchen sink and counters, gathering up the few papers left on my desk and stashing them in a drawer, brushing down a stray cobweb from the living-room ceiling. Then suddenly, the wait is over. There is a knock on the door. The father, a pleasant, bearded man, appears, and behind him is the real Shawna we've all been waiting for.

She is pert and friendly, her dark hair shiny, her eyes bright and direct. I watch Jacob as he says his first hello. He is in heaven. And even though I know that he will suffer from his first love, that this is only one of many steps that will take him away from me—and my protection—I also know it is the beginning of a journey that will make him a man.

I stand back during the initial flurry of hugs and incoherent greetings, and then it's my turn. I step forward, take her hand and smile. "Shawna," I say. "I'm so glad you're here."

Strangely enough, I find I am.

CAROL FEWELL

THE TATTOOED STRANGER

He was scary. He sat there on the grass with his cardboard sign, his dog (actually, his dog was adorable), and tattoos running up and down both arms and even on his neck. His sign proclaimed him to be "stuck and hungry" and asked you to please help.

I'm a sucker for anyone needing help. My husband both loves and hates this quality in me. It often makes him uptight, and I knew if he saw me right now, he'd be nervous. But he wasn't with me right now.

I pulled the van over and in my rearview mirror, contemplated this man, tattoos and all. He was youngish, maybe forty. He wore one of those bandannas tied over his head, biker/pirate style. Anyone could see he was dirty and had a scraggly beard. But if you looked closer, you could see that he had neatly tucked in the black T-shirt, and his things were in a small, tidy bundle. Nobody was stopping for him. I could see the other drivers take one look and immediately focus on something else—anything else.

It was so hot out. I could see in the man's very blue eyes how dejected and tired and worn-out he felt. The sweat was trickling down his face. As I sat with the air-conditioning blowing, the Scripture suddenly popped into my head. "Inasmuch as ye have done it unto one of the least of these, my brethren, so ye have done it unto me."

I reached down into my purse and extracted a ten-dollar bill. My twelve-year-old son, Nick, knew right away what I was doing. "Can I take it to him, Mom?"

"Be careful, honey," I warned, and handed him the money. I watched in the mirror as he rushed over to the man, and with a shy smile, handed it to him. I saw the man, startled, stand up and take the money, putting it into his back pocket. *Good,* I thought to myself, *now he will at least have a hot meal tonight.* I felt satisfied, proud of myself. I had made a sacrifice and now I could go on with my errands.

When Nick got back into the car, he looked at me with sad, pleading eyes. "Mom, his dog looks so hot and the man is really nice." I knew I had to do more.

"Go back and tell him to stay there, that we will be back in fifteen minutes," I told Nick. He bounded out of the car and ran to tell the tattooed stranger. I could see the man was surprised, but nodded his agreement. From my car, my heart did a little flip-flop of excitement.

We then ran to the nearest store and bought our gifts carefully. "It can't be too heavy," I explained to the children. "He has to be able to carry it around with him." We finally settled on our purchases. A bag of "Ol' Roy" (I hoped it was good—it looked good enough for me to eat! How do they make dog food look that way?); a flavored chew toy shaped like a bone; a water dish; bacon-flavored snacks (for the dog); two bottles of water (one for the dog, one for Mr. Tattoos); and some people snacks for the man.

We rushed back to the spot where we had left him, and there he was, still waiting. And still nobody else was stopping for him. With hands shaking, I grabbed our bags and climbed out of the car, all four of my children following me, each carrying gifts. As we walked up to him, I had a fleeting moment of fear, hoping he wasn't a serial killer.

I looked into his eyes and saw something that startled me and made me ashamed of my judgment. I saw tears. He was fighting like a little boy to hold back his tears. How long had it been since someone showed this man kindness? I told him I hoped it wasn't too heavy for him to carry and showed him what we had brought. He stood there, like a child at Christmas, and I felt like my small contributions were so inadequate. When I took out the water dish, he snatched it out of my hands as if it was solid gold and told me he had had no way to give his dog water. He gingerly set it down, filled it with the bottled water we had brought, and stood up to look directly into my eyes. His were so blue, so intense, and my own watered up as he said, "Ma'am, I don't know what to say." He then put both hands on his bandanna-clad head and just started to cry. This man, this "scary" man, was so gentle, so sweet, and so humble.

I smiled and said, "Don't say anything." Then I noticed the tattoo on his neck. It said, "Mama tried."

As we all piled into the van and drove away, he was on his knees, arms around his dog, kissing his nose and smiling. I waved cheerfully and then fully broke down in tears.

I have so much. My worries seem so trivial and petty now. I have a home, a loving husband, and four beautiful children. I have a bed. I wondered where he would sleep tonight.

My stepdaughter, Brandie, turned to me and said in the sweetest little-girl voice, "I feel so good."

Although it seemed as if we had helped him, the man with the tattoos gave us a gift that I will never forget. He taught that no matter what the outside looks like, inside each of us is a human being deserving of kindness, of compassion, of acceptance. He opened my heart.

Tonight and every night I will pray for the gentle man with the tattoos and his dog. And I will hope that God sends more people like him into my life to remind me that love is all there is.

SUSAN FARR-FAHNCKE

COMIC RELIEF

Is that a comic book in my new husband's hand? Comics are for kids, aren't they? The expression of pure concentration on his face piqued my curiosity, though. "What are you reading?"

"The Phantom." Ralph kept his gaze on the book.

"As in, kids Phantom? The guy in the purple suit?"

"That's the one." His eyes stayed focused on the page. When I approached he pulled the comic to his chest. "What?"

"Nothing," I said, and laughed. "How come you're reading The Phantom?"

"I like it." His frown deepened, and his brown eyes shifted back and forth. "Anything wrong with that?"

Sensing his mood, I backed off. "No. You go ahead."

Later that week I found him hunched over the comic at his desk. I was sure I heard him mumbling.

"Ralph, what's wrong?" I placed my hand on his shoulder and heard him sigh. I glanced down at the black-and-white pictures. He was on the same page as before. He slid his elbow across the open comic and looked up at me, a strange expression on his face.

"I don't read so good," he mumbled, lowering his head. "It takes me a long time to get through one of these." Not knowing what to say, I watched his face. The man I loved was worrying over my response. Smiling, I hugged him and asked, "How come?" He tried to break away from my arms, but I held tight. "How come you can't read so good?"

He went on to tell me, tears streaming down his face, about

his upbringing. About how his mother insisted he was brain-damaged, and about his failed education. Forced to sit in a slow learners class, Ralph learned nothing from a teacher with an anything-goes attitude. A couple of his church mates taught him basic words before we'd met. So now he could read very small, un-complicated words. The comics were perfect, because he could work out the story by studying the pictures and from the few words he knew. Admitting this to me hurt his pride deeply. In his eyes, it made him less of a man. It simply made me love him more.

Around this time a friend asked Ralph to teach Sunday school at church. At first he refused, saying he lacked the necessary skills to prepare weekly lessons. After much persistence, though, he reluctantly gave in to the pleas. Another friend took Ralph into the city, purchased an expensive Bible, and presented it to him, then painstakingly showed him how to prepare a Sunday school lesson.

Each Saturday Ralph spent hours crafting his lessons. Usually this involved borderline curses, pen-throwing, and threats to quit. I tiptoed around the house, making myself available when asked. "Heather, how do you spell HOW?"

"H-O-W."

Ten minutes later. "Heather, how do you spell HOW?"

"H-O-W."

I wanted to shout, "I just told you how to spell HOW." Still, I kept quiet and waited for the next word. I became a living dictio-nary. Usually the words he needed were more complicated. He met my quiet offers of instruction or explaining rules of grammar with cool glares and, "I just want to know how to spell it."

He'd attempt to read items in the newspaper or personal let-ters, slowly pronouncing the words in the obvious fashion in which they presented themselves. If I offered any suggestions, he'd ignore me and press on. His barely concealed frustration would give way and with a loud sigh he'd shove the item at me to read. He began to hold on to the page more often, though, and jab a finger at offending words, asking between clenched teeth, "What does that word say?"

I'd read the word out and he'd repeat it. If I mistook the direction of his finger and read the wrong word, he'd say, "That word, there," underlining with another finger jab. Even though he struggled to contain his anger, he always thanked me. Over time I learned not to be so sensitive, no longer assuming he was angry with me. Conquering words was a daily challenge for him.

Communication is tough for most newlyweds, but it was tougher for us than most. He'd often misunderstand my intentions and meanings, and me his. I believe it made us work harder. We spent hours awake in bed long after retiring for the night. With the darkness shrouding our reservations, we talked, shared, cried, and laughed together.

All the while, I purchased Phantom comics for him. I stacked them on bench tops, his bedside table, anywhere he would see them. Whenever I read a book, he'd pick up a Phantom and immerse himself in the simple story line. It was companionable, and I was glad he was reading for pure pleasure. Soon he was reading faster. The chore of preparing lessons each Saturday gradually gave way to delight. Bible study became his passion.

Although my children probably have a higher reading level, as far as education goes, Ralph is now an adequate reader. The Phantom comics strewn about the house ensured that my family became fans of the guy in the purple suit. Ralph can read a comic in an afternoon, and has learned to be gracious about any help I offer. He allows me to laugh at his mistakes because he now understands the humor and subtle beauty found in words.

Sometimes he looks over his Sunday school lessons and marvels how the kids ever learned anything from him. Even he struggles now to understand the words written on those yellowing pages. I know he'll never part with them. They are trophies for the boy within who didn't learn to read. He prizes those indecipherable lessons because they measure his progress.

Just as he cherishes those lessons, I hold dear a Valentine card he once made for me. It reads, "I luv yu, my sweat haret."

HEATHER GOLDSMITH

We can only learn to love by loving.
IRIS MURDOCH

THAT FEELING CALLED LOVE

My daughter proudly handed me the small bundle, and I could feel the tension shooting through me. I looked into the tiny face, surrounded by dark hair, and thought, *I'm a grandmother. Why don't I feel like one?* What was wrong with me, why wasn't I experiencing the delight I'd heard other grandmothers talk about? Why did I tremble instead, feeling clumsy and unsure of how to hold my own grandson?

As the months passed and Bradie grew older, I began to relax, although I did find myself checking on him frequently during the nights he stayed at our home. He was always all right, yet I continued to feel inadequate as a grandma. Would I ever feel joy instead?

Soon, Bradie was walking, and before long he was chatting up a storm, not that we could determine what was being said. He began spending more time with his grandfather and me. I could see his personality evolving as he struggled with speech. We read his favorite books and built castles out of corrugated cardboard to house the numerous Ninja Turtles and other assorted plastic monsters he'd acquired.

He had sleepovers at our home to which he brought his favorite long, skinny rabbit, Bob, and eventually when Bradie was three and a half years old, his imaginary friend, Mogli. For the next six months, Mogli and Bradie were the Velcro twins. "Don't sit on Mogli," he'd say. Or "Mogli's hungry, too, Grandma." Occasionally, Mogli was blamed for some naughty deed. Most often, though, Mogli was quiet and well-behaved.

I began looking forward to the time that I spent with Bradie, arranging my workload so that I picked him up Friday nights after my job as a bookkeeper. He had turned four and his interests were expanding. Together we would dream up ideas for stories. "Let's put a dragon in the story," he'd say. "And I'll save the town from it. Me and my friend Bob." After I'd take him home, I'd work at my computer, twisting and turning the words to form the excitement Bradie had come to expect from one of "our" stories. It delighted me to delight him. And it warmed my heart when I'd stop by and he'd pull one of "our" books from the bookshelf for me to read.

Soon after Bradie began playschool, we noticed that his discussions with his imaginary friend, Mogli, were becoming further and further apart until finally they stopped altogether. He was suddenly interested in making things; but as he had the attention span of a four-year old, any project that tended to be lengthy ended up being completed by Grandma herself. To avoid this problem, I searched for simple children's crafts, then worked with Bradie to assemble the projects, giving him the satisfaction of a job well done. "Look what I made," he'd tell his mother joyfully. "I made it just for you." And I would smile—my heart full of love for this special little person who graced my life.

As summer nears, I've begun thinking of the beauty of the Rocky Mountains, the blue sky, the clear, cool streams, and the pine-scented air. I'm getting the itch to go camping. There's nothing better than that, I think, as I drive Bradie home after one of our special times. Unless, of course, it's seeing all those things, like new, through the eyes of my grandson.

"I love to come to your house, Grandma," he tells me as we pull into his driveway and he scrambles from my car. "You're the best Grandma in the whole wide world." I grin, blinking back the tears that burn the backs of my eyes. Yes. There's something about that boy that's really gotten to me. And that feeling called love sweeps over me again. But then . . . isn't that the way all grandmothers feel?

CHRIS MIKALSON

WATCHING REAL BEAUTY

I was sitting in a diner, enjoying my solitude and absorbed in thoughts of my father. It was the anniversary of his death and I was missing him.

From the corner of my eye, I noticed a magnificent-looking couple in a nearby booth. The woman was incredibly beautiful, with large, dark, seductive eyes, thick black hair pulled sleekly into a French knot, and an airbrushed complexion. Her movements were fluid. She was poised and composed and appeared to be detached from her surroundings. I watched as she sipped her coffee, and I realized that hers were the looks I'd always wanted.

The man was gorgeous. I stared shamelessly and smiled to myself as I allowed my fantasies to ramble. His skin was tanned, and he had rugged features with a strong cleft chin and clear blue eyes. The cut of his expensive three-piece suit accentuated his broad chest and shoulders.

He was reading a newspaper. She was drinking coffee. They never spoke.

I heard myself sigh and tried to pull my thoughts back to where they had been before they were so pleasantly invaded. It was difficult. I was drawn to the two of them and their robotlike movements—turning his pages, lifting her cup. No speaking. No smiling. No communicating.

My thoughts were further interrupted when the hostess escorted another couple to a booth diagonally in front of mine. They appeared to be frequent patrons of the diner because they joked with the waitress, who asked if they wanted their "usual."

The man was in his mid-sixties. His hair was steel gray and he wore baggy shorts that slung low on his hips, inviting his belly to hang over. He wore a horizontally striped polo shirt and a red billed cap. Black dress shoes and short black socks accentuated his thin, white, bowed legs.

The woman, about fifty-five, had short frizzy brown hair with long gray roots. She wore plaid Bermuda shorts, a sleeveless polka dot overblouse, white sandals with white anklets, and carried a small white patent leather handbag. She had no forearms. Finger-like appendages hung from her elbows.

I tried hard to ignore her deformity but found myself sneaking peeks at her reflection in the window alongside me. Distance made their conversation inaudible to me, but their perpetual dialogue, laughter, and playful animation revealed the warmth and the depth of their feelings for each other.

I stalled by reordering cups of tea. I was intrigued by the contrast in the appearance and behavior of the two couples.

The beautiful people slid across their booth seats, stood, and prepared to leave. I observed that the woman was tall and willowy. The man appeared to be about six-five and, in my humble opinion, was a perfect specimen of manhood. The woman walked in front of the man, past the cashier, and out the door. He paid the check and followed. They never spoke or so much as acknowledged each other's presence. They were perfectly sculpted pieces of cold marble.

I was on my third cup of tea by now and feeling uncomfortable about lingering any longer when the second couple stood and prepared to leave. When he reached the woman's side of the table, the man leaned over and whispered something into her ear, causing her to visibly blush and giggle. They embraced. I hid behind my menu and softly cried.

They were walking toward the cashier when the man suddenly turned and came back to his booth. He reached across the seat on which he'd been sitting and came up with his red cap.

My eyes were still moist as I managed a smile and said, "Good thing you remembered it now, instead of after you were on the road."

He grinned broadly and walked over to me. "See this here pin?" he asked with great pride as he pointed to a small brass heart stuck in his cap. "My wife gave it to me over forty years ago and I'm never without it."

I smiled approvingly and he returned to the cashier where he paid his check and walked out with his arm over his woman's shoulders.

As my eyes followed them to the parking lot, memories of my father trickled back into my mind and I was struck with thoughts of something he had told me when I was a youngster working beside him in his roadside fruit and vegetable stand. "The sweetest fruits are often the ones with blemishes and imperfections."

I was warmed by thoughts of my father's words and realized that while the beautiful people had caught my eye, it was the second couple who had captured my heart.

LAVERNE BARDY POLLAK

A MIRACLE
OF MY OWN

I *started out in life with an eye for the miraculous. Soon, how-*
ever, disappointment marred my vision.

One Sunday, I stood up in church, where my mother
found miracles weekly, and waited for the minister to lay hands
on me for healing. You could go up front for any type of healing, physical or spiritual, and I think I wanted a bit of both. You
see, my heart was heavy with grief that year. Our family had
been scattered like leaves in the wind, victims of a storm called
divorce, and the sadness made me sick to my stomach most of the
time.

All around me, dewy-skinned believers were passing out like
drunks under the power of the Holy Spirit traveling through
the minister's hands. As soon as Pastor Jim touched their fore-
heads and pronounced them healed-in-the-name-of-Jesus, out
they went. Falling back, they found the waiting hands of an usher,
who gently laid them out on their backs. They lay there, eyes
closed, lips trembling, hands folded, looking like Rapture itself. I
wanted some of that.

Tingling with excitement, I waited for my turn. Finally, Pastor
Jim stood before me. He reached his hands toward my bowed
head, and I noticed the soft scent of something that smelled holy
emanating from his long delicate fingers. Pastor put his hands on
my forehead. He spoke the healing words. As "Jesus" rolled off his
tongue, he pushed. I took a small step back, felt the waiting hands
of the faithful usher on my back, and then regained my balance.

Undaunted, the minister tried once more. Again, he pronounced me healed. Again, he tried to push me down.

I refused to go.

I felt bad, standing there. I wanted to belong, wanted to feel rapture, wanted to be healed. But I did *not* want to be pushed.

"He tried to push me down," I muttered as we drove home, disappointment settling heavily in my chest. Mom just looked at me with soft pity gleaming in her eyes. I never again mentioned the incident, fearing that somehow I was to blame, that I was unworthy, or that I lacked the necessary faith to experience the supernatural.

But recently, I have been healed. My eye for the miraculous—restored.

On the last weekend of summer, I stood at the picture window that overlooks our backyard, eyes locked on an inviting patch of green grass. The yard slopes slightly at one corner, and is the perfect place to enjoy a backyard picnic, or to sit and watch the ants trying to find their way home. Temptation washed over me. The sense of longing I felt to spread a blanket and lie in the sun became unbearable. So I ignored the pile of laundry that screamed to be washed and the creaking floor that begged to be swept—I grabbed a blanket and my book and dashed outside.

"Only a half hour or so," I murmured to myself. "Just for a while, since the kids are napping."

On the rock patio, I paused to enjoy the sigh of a warm breeze whispering through my hair. I recognized the delicate aroma of smoke in the air. Delicious campfire smoke. My mouth watered with the memory of marshmallows toasted golden brown on sticks.

I walked toward the waiting lawn. My *feet* went elsewhere.

The dreamy patch of grass beckoned to me from my left, but my feet went right . . . into the side yard where I never go.

The side yard is mostly dirt, and mostly shaded by the house and the giant fir tree that stands there. My husband had been outside the day before and had raked the dry leaves and twigs into small neat piles, leaving in the dirt the graceful curving lines reminiscent of Buddhist meditative sand painting. I smiled at the pattern, then spread my blanket in a patch of sun, careful not to disturb the simple beauty of my husband's work. The scent of pine rose from the earth like steam from a batch of freshly baked cookies. Hungrily, I inhaled the scent, then settled in to read.

Smoke again. This time stronger, less like campfire smoke, more like danger. Looking up from my book, now I saw the smoke. I followed its trail and found, hidden from plain sight by a few strategically placed azaleas and a rotting tree stump, a bold fire burning.

Fire!

Right in my side yard—where I never go—and out of view from any windows of the house, a fire burned in the midday light. Five large buckets of water were required to douse the fire. Afterward, I raked the pile of scorched yard debris and found smoldering embers still glowing. Two more buckets, and I knew it was out. Standing there, I stared at the large black spot that remained. My eyes traveled quickly from the burned spot to the fence, to the rotting tree stump; then from dry bush to dry bush, over to the side of the house, and up to the window of the room where my children slept. Smoke had drifted into their open window, and I felt sure it had coated their dreams in campfire glory.

Then and there, I redefined *miracle* and made it my very own.

I marvel at the car accidents I haven't been in, the diseases I don't have, and at the fire that didn't destroy property or threaten the lives of my children. Most of all, I marvel at my restored ability to *perceive* the miracles—which are sometimes as shy as shooting stars on clear summer nights.

Now, I realize that most preachers don't push people down.

And I believe that power and wonder really touched those people, and I'm glad.

But as for me, I now experience the Divine on a different scale—I am seeing the miracles that are meant just for me.

LUCI N. FULLER

II
GATHERING WISDOM

One of the gifts of being human is the wisdom we gather within.

It's a feeling we can draw from for all eternity.

<small>JENNIFER JAMES</small>

FIRST PANCAKE OUT OF THE FRYING PAN

First children are like the first pancake out of the frying pan: mushy in the middle and a little crispy around the edges. The rest of the batch are evenly browned and cooked all the way through, but that first one usually suffers. So you toss it onto your garage roof for the birds, and they think it's just fine. The rest of the pancakes give you much less trouble.

But that's pancakes. As much as I was occasionally tempted, I never once tossed my firstborn child onto the garage roof. I struggled on with his sensitive soul and with the macho exterior because of course I was awfully fond of him, even with syrup all over his face, hands, shirt, and the floor.

But here's the thing. He will forever be my first child. Not just when he was little and I chafed at his twelve-minute naps, his temper tantrums because he couldn't create perfection with Lego blocks, his insistence on eating only Froot Loops and hot dogs, and his refusal to share the Ernie puppet with his sister. He is destined to be my first pancake . . . forever.

He was my first child to play at a friend's house. Did I know that house was childproofed? Did I know that the other mother would have Froot Loops? I did not—and it required a great leap of faith to leave him there.

He was the first to escape through his bedroom window at 9:00 P.M. to try to steal a Big Wheel from the front porch of people who didn't know him. Not yet old enough to talk, it required ingenuity for them to figure out where he belonged.

He was the first to teach me that bribery with M&Ms works just fine, thank you, especially when applied to potty training. He was the first to lose a new jacket, the first to cross the street alone, and the first to spend two years of swimming lessons showing us how determined he was not to swim.

My son, my first pancake, showed me the strength of a child's clothing preferences. On the hottest day of the year, he insisted on wearing hiking boots, heavy corduroy pants, a long-sleeved turtleneck shirt, and a belt pulled so tightly that his eyeballs bulged. We fought like two bobcats in a bag, me trying to wrestle him into shorts, he holding stubbornly to his conviction that only in this particular outfit would he feel properly dressed.

When his sister came along a few years later and wore the same green sweater every day for eighteen months, I barely noticed. And I would have let my third child go to school in his Pooh Bear jammies if he'd wanted to. It would have saved on the laundry.

Then came the biggie, the one every parent dreads.

My firstborn learned to drive.

The day he got his license, he asked to take his sister and brother for a ride around the block. I agreed, but as he pulled away from the curb, I yelled, "You have all of my children in that car!"

When half an hour had passed, I called the police, but my son arrived just as the squad car pulled up. He'd become trapped in a freeway on-ramp and had driven ten miles before getting up the nerve to exit, turn around, and come home.

He never knew how close he came to being tossed onto the garage roof that day.

As a teenager he swung from a branch that broke and smashed the window in a baby's bedroom next door. We grounded him for the rest of the weekend. As I walked past his room Sunday afternoon, he growled, "I should be helping Dad fix that window instead of lying here listening to Madonna."

When I paused, he said I probably didn't know the first thing about appropriate discipline of teenagers.

Kicking my way through mountains of T-shirts, I prepared to deliver a lecture based on nothing more than my authority as Mom. But suddenly I saw the situation through his eyes: a teenager dealing with the first-time mother of a teenager.

I realized that we're taking this trip together. Everything I was saying to him could be applied to me as well. As he is my first child, he must suffer through the effects of my first tries at parenting. But so must I deal with each particular stage he goes through for the first time, and here's the hard part: I must do it based on no experience whatsoever.

So I apologized for the fact that we were each other's first pancakes. Each of his stages is virgin territory for both of us. Together we are learning to navigate in the unmapped wilderness of his path toward adulthood.

I leaned forward and smiled at him. "Look, could you cut me a little slack here? I don't know what I'm doing any more than you do, but you're always going to be the first one through each of these stages, and that's just the way it is. If you think there's something I should know that would make my job easier, please, share it with me. I need all the help I can get."

He looked at me a long moment, and then his jaw relaxed and the corners of his mouth struggled with his lips, all twitching and curving as his eyes crinkled. And then he laughed.

I think it was the first time he saw me as Mom, the struggling pancake maker, rather than as Mother, the perfect cook, goddess of all knowledge and kitchen wisdom.

Both of us liked Mom the best.

PEGGY VINCENT

Serenity is not freedom from the storm but *peace within the storm.*
AUTHOR UNKNOWN

MORE THAN PIZZA

What began like any other Monday-night staff meeting soon took a bizarre twist. "Hello . . . yes, I'd like to order two medium pizzas, with a two-liter bottle of Coke. Yes, that's to 2695 Hanover Pike—" I was cut off by a male's voice on the other end of the phone. "Is this a church?" "Yes it is," I answered. "Sorry lady, I don't deliver to churches," he responded crisply.

This had to be some sort of joke. Someone was playing a prank. After all, we'd held staff meetings on Monday night for years and ordered pizza from this particular place. We also have a school at the church and pizzas are ordered on a regular basis because of all the activities that go on in our building.

I informed him that we'd been frequent customers. "Lady, I don't care who did what before, I'm the manager here tonight, and I told you that I don't deliver to churches. Whether you get a pizza tonight will depend on whether I can get another driver to deliver it." Totally stunned, all I could stammer out was, "May I ask why?" He snapped back, "Because I don't like churches, that's why!" "Well, that's too bad sir, because obviously you have never heard of our church, where people love and care for one another."

With my quick yet pleasant retort, I evidently pushed him a little over the edge, and he angrily snapped back, "Will that be hand-tossed or deep-dish?" "Deep-dish," I replied. "It'll be there in thirty minutes," he said, and literally slammed the phone down.

I quickly filled everyone in on my bizarre conversation, and we settled in for our meeting. We were engrossed in conversation when we heard the driver pull up outside. One of the staff members went out in the hallway to get the door and pay him.

Several seconds later I heard voices outside my office door. I could hear a familiar voice saying, "What I said on the phone was really uncalled for. I felt I should come here and apologize in person to the woman I spoke to on the telephone."

Immediately I stood up from my desk, came out into the hallway, and extended my hand. Warmly receiving it, he said, "Hello, my name is James, and I want to personally apologize for my behavior on the phone." I smiled and said, "Hi James, my name is Pastor Deanna, and it's a privilege to meet you, and . . . your apology is accepted." He softened a bit and said, "I don't know what got into me when you called tonight. I've been going through a hard time. My little girl recently died, and now my wife is leaving me. I'm in a lot of pain, and right now, I'm mad at God. To me, church represents God. That's why I reacted like I did when you called, but that was no excuse. My behavior was unacceptable, and I'm so sorry."

My heart really went out to this man. Lending a comforting ear, the staff had by this time gathered with us in the hallway, and we were listening to James as he talked, offering sympathy and, if he desired it, prayer. He maintained that right now no one could understand his pain. Knowing the backgrounds of those in that circle, including myself, I offered, "James, some of us really do understand your pain. We have been through many trials ourselves and have had much to overcome in life. We understand hurt and pain, and we really want to help you."

Toughening back up a bit, he looked me square in the eye, pointed a finger, and said, "Lady, you would never, never, understand my pain in a million years! It goes way beyond my wife and daughter. Nobody can understand the root of my pain." At that, he backed away, and stared out the hallway window with a cynical look in his eyes. "Try me!" I shot back. Without missing a beat, he stepped forward again, raised his finger and said, voice breaking, "Do you know what it's like to have your mother abandon you as a child? To give you up for adoption? Do you know what it's like to never know the woman who birthed you, and gave you life? Do you know what it's like to have brothers and sisters and relatives that you have never met, somewhere on this earth, but you don't know them? Do you know what it's like to look into people's faces every day and wonder if they are related to you somehow? Do you know what it's like to search for these people for years and never find them, and have a void in your life that won't be filled until you do? Do you?" His voice got more passionate and angry as tears welled up in his eyes.

Meanwhile, my staff and I were trying hard not to cry, or break out laughing, because James had just described my life story, exactly. My mother gave me up for adoption as a child, and I also had a birth brother and sister. For the first twenty-seven years, there was that void in my life of "not knowing." I searched for thirteen years to find them, and with God's help, did so in 1993. I had been through all the same things James had described, and more—and perhaps most important, I had come through on the other side. All of us realized that we were encountering a divine appointment. There was something sacred about this moment.

I looked him back—square in the eye—and said, "Yes, I do know exactly how that feels, James, for you have just described my life." I was able to sympathize and, as time went on, offered him practical help in finding his birth family. I stayed in contact with James as he continued to deliver pizzas to the church, and he let me in on how he was doing with all the challenges in his life.

God knew in His divine plan that a pizza deliveryman and a pastor needed to cross paths that night. I've come to learn that divine appointments await us at every turn if we just look for them. I shudder to think of what would have happened had I angrily hung up the phone on James and ordered pizza from another place. We would have both missed a holy encounter that affected us for life. What a wonderful reminder to me that our Creator keeps tabs on us all and knows just what we need and when.

DEANNA DOSS SHRODES

A willing heart adds feather to the heel.
JOANNA BAILLE

EDDIE'S FATHER

I had known Eddie's father since our Crying Room days. We were bunched together in the small, soundproof room in the back of our church where parents sit with noisy babies.

Eight years later, our sons were playing against each other in a Little League Midget Division game. I hadn't noticed Eddie's dad until I heard a shout coming from the sideline.

"What's a big kid like that doing out there?"

I looked over to see Eddie's dad pointing at my son, Christian, who was the pitcher. At the moment, Christian's team happened to be leading Eddie's team.

Years went by. The few times our paths crossed, we both avoided eye contact. Then one day, I was chaperoning my daughter Katherine's high-school basketball team to an away game, and was surprised to see Eddie's dad driving the bus. Once we arrived at the game arena, I was surprised again when he told the ticket-taker that I was the "assistant coach" so I wouldn't have to pay the gate fee.

After the game, all the girls went home with the parents who had attended. It was just Katherine and Eddie's father and me on the bus for the hour-long drive home. Katherine promptly fell asleep. I was unwilling to face the long drive staring into blackness, so I moved up to the seat behind the driver.

I thanked him for his kindness at the ticket booth. We chatted about our families, and the miles flew by. At one point, he commented how great it was for our town that Christian had made it as a professional athlete. I took that opening to ask the question that had been on my mind for eighteen years.

"Do you remember that Little League game when you yelled about Christian's size? How come you did that when you knew he was the same age as Eddie?"

"You know," he answered, "that has bothered me for a long time. I realized my mistake a few years later when Christian was twelve years old and playing on the same team as Eddie. It had rained hard the night before. I was first-base coach. Christian singled. Then he got onto second on the next batter, and I'll never forget this: When I looked in his direction, there was Christian, all six-feet-two of him, kneeling on the ground, making mud pies. After that, for all these years, I've wanted to say I was sorry."

BONITA (BONNIE) LAETTNER

IF GRANDMOTHERS RAN
THE WORLD

*S*ometimes it feels like the world is falling apart. My solution is to put grandmothers in charge.

In my family, grandmothers enjoy the most unique and prominent position in the clan. I know I wouldn't think of turning a deaf ear to what Mama Hudson said, or for that matter denying her persuasive power.

After all, who else but the family matriarch determines the fate of the family traditions, decides which dish each brings to the reunions, dictates the details of weddings, funerals, holiday get-togethers, christenings, bar mitzvahs, engagement parties, birthday celebrations, graduations of any ilk, long-term illnesses, or family vacations? Grandmother, that's who.

If governments tapped into this powerful secret weapon, mankind would take a giant step toward global peace. Just the thought of silver-haired grannies from all races, backgrounds, faiths, and nations meeting on common issues makes me warm all over.

Grandmothers are bold. Helen, my children's grandmother, overcame her fear of flying only to board a jet and traverse the ocean to Africa for a glimpse of her new granddaughter. Granny Smith raised a large brood battling the Depression and world war. She could have converted Mussolini with her southern fried chicken, cathead biscuits, and homemade pear preserves.

With grandmothers at the governmental helm, heads of state might swap family recipes and tips for removing grape juice stains from carpet instead of looking for terrorists. There wouldn't be any terrorists. Government heads could do battle in the kitchen instead of on battlegrounds. We would witness a world where coupons and quilt blocks are exchanged instead of gunfire. Peace negotiations could be enhanced with a nice salad luncheon/fashion show. All grandmothers invited—RSVP required.

Grandmothers are wise. My paternal grandmother, Sally Mae, was the one the family turned to when they needed an assist with a newborn, a crisis, or a death. She took care of a new mother, paced with a colicky infant, or prepared chicken and dumplings for the flu sufferer. She was tireless, opinionated, comforting, smelling of flowers, brimming with stories, and armed with a prayer life.

The grandmothers in my life are beautiful no matter what size or shape. Young or old, thin or rotund, wearing bifocals or running marathons. The only requirement is to possess a hearty laugh and a hug that says, "Everything will be all right."

With their wisdom and tender loving care, grandmothers could easily run the world. The position of grandparenting would be elevated. Young women would aspire to such heights and look forward to aging with grace and beauty. Grandmothering would be a much-valued art and accorded supermodel status. Grandmother politicians would debate prep schools while proudly sharing the latest photos of grand- and great-grandchildren. Professor grandmothers would not dye their hair, but rather glory in silver tresses earned from a full life. College credit would be awarded to grandmothers for life experience and self-shaped philosophy.

The Grandmother-President-in-Charge, which could have been aptly filled by my feisty great-grandmother Davis, who held off Yankees from a dormer window, would organize a tour of third world countries complete with cooking classes, mothering lectures, sewing lessons, and quilting bees. Each third Thursday would be declared an idea/cookie swap with childcare and refreshments provided.

If grandmothers ran the world, senior citizens would be recognized as vibrant contributors to society. Baby-sitters would be out of a job, daycare facilities would stand empty, and family counselors would have to take part-time jobs. Barbecue sauce would flow like water and children would never feel so secure.

Bosnian and Serbian grandmothers would resolve differences over high tea. Mexican and U.S. grandmothers would oversee adoptions, with children winning all the way around. European grandmothers would agree on borders and currency while Asian grandmothers would share secrets of origami and healthy cooking tips. World powers would encourage faith as important to their nation.

The world would sleep easier at night and take a giant step toward Utopia if grandmothers ruled. Granny Chitwood would never have stood for the Holocaust, World Wars I and II, the Korean War, Vietnam, or the Persian Gulf incident. No grandmother worth her title would think of holding hostages, shooting down planes, or making war. She is too busy looking after her household, caring about her community, and making sure everyone is tucked in at night with stories and prayers. A grandmother's courage is aptly displayed in the day-to-day routine of a life well lived.

With grandmothers in charge, this reeling and frazzled world could see a lot of improvements. Mama Sewell always greeted us with "Where's my hugs and where's my kisses?" She waved goodbye with whispers of "sweet dreams," "take care," "call me," and "I love you." When you think of it, it's not a bad way to end any negotiation.

SHEILA S. HUDSON

HOW ARE YOU SMART?

I always knew I was different. While other teens threw themselves into the high-school life, I found it boring and uninspiring. It wasn't that I was a rebellious youth; I just found no point in it. No one could give me an explanation as to why I would need to study higher math when I wasn't even good at lower math. Many of the adults I talked to admitted that they didn't use half the stuff they had learned in high school and had forgotten the other half. I hated most of the classes, I detested the pecking order, and I scorned the pressure to conform.

My parents were hauled in to talk to the counselors more than once, and they all said the same thing. "She reads books during math, she skips science altogether, and she isn't involved in anything. With her test scores, she should be doing exemplary work, and yet she is failing almost everything except psychology and creative writing."

"I like those classes," I remember muttering.

"You don't have to like them, you just have to do it."

No, I don't, I thought. Okay . . . maybe I was rebellious.

But I had goals that had nothing to do with school. One of them was to read every piece of classic literature I could find by the time I was twenty-five. I also wanted to learn more about horses, get a nurse's assistant certificate so that I could work with the elderly, and write a book on old homesteads in eastern Oregon. I wanted to learn to write poetry and become an expert on the roaring twenties. What I loved was education; what I didn't like was school. So, six months before the end of the twelfth grade, I quit.

I remember how excited I was. I was free! Free to learn and study all that the world had to offer. I wanted to spread my wings and fly.

What I ended up with was crushed wings.

"You'll never amount to anything."

"I'm so disappointed."

"My Mom doesn't want me hanging out with you anymore."

"I never expected you to be a dropout."

Dropout. Dropout equals Loser.

What little self-esteem I had left from years of failing at the school social scene, I lost that first year after I left. I allowed people to define me by a piece of paper. I knew they were wrong. I knew I was better-educated than many of those who had diplomas, but I was tired of fighting.

I lost something precious that year. I came to doubt every decision I made and because of that, ended up making some very bad ones. I married the wrong man, I moved to the wrong places, I took the wrong jobs.

By the time I was twenty-three I was burnt out, defeated, and perpetually sad. I cringed every time I had to fill out a job application and had to mark "No" under high-school diploma—knowing that people would classify and categorize me. I masked this inferiority with parties and alcohol, and I despaired of ever finding that fearless girl who left school to learn again.

But I did.

I left my husband, who had succumbed to alcoholism, and met and married a man who saw the intelligent woman lurking beneath the frightened child.

Marrying him was the first good choice I had made in years. I followed that up by choosing to have two beautiful children. I was on a roll now! I gained confidence with every year, and when they were old enough to go to school, I desperately wanted to educate them at home.

I remember whispering my longing and doubt to my husband late at night.

"I want to, but should I?"

"You should," he whispered back.

"But could I?"

"You can."

It turned out to be the best choice we could have made, for both my children and myself.

We made our little school an enchanted place of learning. I watched while they learned to count and rejoiced when they learned to read. While we studied Indians and frontiersmen, we made clay pots, sewed (fake) raccoon caps, and went to numerous museums to study frontier weapons. We studied biology by discovering the starfish, crabs, and unique plants that inhabit tide pools. We raised tadpoles in our small pond, watching with delight as they developed into tiny, perfect frogs. We spent hours at the library until they knew the librarians by name, and I was reminded of the secret fascination the library always held for me. We now volunteer at that same library, checking books in, shelving, and setting up special events.

Slowly, while teaching my children, I regained not only my love of learning, but also the confidence that I could learn and do anything I set my mind to. And in modeling that for our children, I hope to give them that same priceless gift. I want them to know that no matter what sort of schooling a person receives, education is something you must do for yourself, not something that is done to you.

One day we were at the park and I happened to hear a conversation my son was having with another boy. The boy asked my son where he went to school at. My son replied that he was home-schooled.

"My mom says that you can't do anything if you don't have a high-school diploma," the other boy told him scornfully.

"Yes, you can," my son corrected. "Look at my mom, she doesn't have one and she can do lots and lots of things. Not having a diploma didn't stop her."

I thought of all the things I have done and learned, how beautiful and intelligent my children are, and how much success I am having at my chosen career. "No," I whispered softly, "it hasn't stopped me."

TERI BROWN

I'm looking forward to looking back on all this.
SANDRA KNELL

GETTING THE PICTURE

Last year I didn't get my Christmas card out until the end of January. It all started with the picture. My husband suggested I take my own. I was inspired. I enjoy photography, and this would be a nice little project to fill my "idle" hours.

I approached my photographic mission with zeal. The very next morning, I got the kids decked out in matching Christmas garb, itself no small task. But my children's agenda that morning was not my agenda. I wanted them to sit primly posed and smile adorably for me, keeping eyes open, drool off faces, and thumbs out of mouths. All at the same time. The agenda of my two-year-old twins was to sit for two seconds, spit, drool, hop, bounce, jump, run away, stand on their heads, and then catch their six-month-old brother's neck in a stranglehold.

If the girls did, by chance, stop acting as if they had just had a run-in with a cattle prod and sit down for a moment, they would stare at me glumly, listlessly, looking depressed and refusing to smile. This would go on until my baby would actually burst into tears, Brittany's finger would be pensively inserted into her nose, and Holly's thumb would pop vacuously into her mouth. It just wasn't working. I started feeling just a little frustrated.

So I decided to take them outside. We all needed a change of scenery. The day was warm. The light was good. A lot of leaves were down in the backyard, and I hoped they might serve as a good distraction. Perhaps my offspring would be so engrossed in the beauty and intricacy of the leaves, they would stop to contemplate the meaning of life, and while they were doing so, I could snap a few prize pictures. Then we'd all be satisfied.

They were, indeed, engrossed. The baby commenced stuffing leaves into his face at an alarming rate, as if he was some human form of a tough-enough-to-overstuff Hefty garbage bag. The girls contemplated the meaning of life while performing an interpretive dance of free ions in a gaseous state. At this point, I knew I should really just put my camera away and give up. Walk away. But this had become more than just getting a little Christmas picture. This had become more about my ability to get something done, to follow through, to make things happen.

We had recently moved out of state, away from friends and family, to a town where we knew nobody. I was staying at home with the kids, and while I loved being a mom, I was, at times, practically desperate to prove to myself that I really had things under control and was "adjusting" well. And a photograph never lies, right?

I could see the desired picture in my mind's eye: A shot that would show the world my happy, well-groomed (did I mention clean?) children laughing and interacting in a meaningful manner. It was a simple goal to capture, on film, the defining essences of each of my three children. In short, to produce for posterity a piece of physical and irrefutable evidence of my mothering abilities.

So I became determined with a grim and joyless determination to get that perfect shot. As my blood pressure rose, I begged, bribed, wheedled, cajoled, demanded, commanded, and practically cried. All to no avail. I couldn't even get them to sit down, let alone to sit still and smile. I grew more frantic, more desperate, with each advance of the film. This was definitely not my plan. Why couldn't they, just once, do what I wanted? Why couldn't they just let me have the small satisfaction of producing one single image that would demonstrate my prowess as a mother, as an organizer, as a woman-in-control? Just one convincing shot. Was this really too much to ask? The pictures I had taken so far would all more likely be worthy of a garbage can than a Christmas card.

It was in this moment of despair that it happened. In the moment that I had just given up. All three kids sat down, looked up and smiled, looked happy, intelligent, and reasonably clean. It wasn't anything I said or did, but it was a Perfect Shot. Composition, light, color, everything. Perfect. The kind of shot where you look in the viewfinder, and you just know, this is going to be one of the best pictures you have ever taken. A chill went up my spine. And here I had almost given up! I pressed the shutter button firmly, feeling a rush of smug triumph. I felt the button go down. And stop. And nothing. No satisfying click of the shutter to consummate my success. Nothing. Silence. Except for my sharply indrawn breath, as I realized I had come to the end of the roll, and had no film left.

I had missed the Greatest Picture of My Life! I knew this said something important, but was too disgusted with myself to care. Fuming, I set my camera aside and sat in the golden sunshine of a late-October day. I sat and just watched my children play. I watched without the need now, or the desire, to capture it, to put a spin on it, to make it anything other than what it really was: two two-year-olds and a baby, experiencing their world, running, chasing, darting, shrieking, hopping, drooling, throwing leaves, laughing. Happy, well-adjusted children interacting in a meaningful manner. Experiencing and enjoying life, not trying to conquer it, force it, or control it. A sort of sacred dance.

I had been on a mission, but as it turns out, so had they—the same mission that all very small children are on: Live for the moment, and enjoy it.

I didn't get the perfect Christmas card shot that day, but I think I did, in fact, get the picture.

KAREN C. DRISCOLL

FINDING CHRISTMAS

"Mom, I called to tell you I won't make it home for Christmas this year."

Shock numbed my heart! This would be the first Christmas in thirty-five years that our family would be separated. Our daughter, pregnant and due to deliver on December 29, was planning a quiet day at home with her husband. And now our son, calling from the other coast, was telling us his recent promotion with the airlines wouldn't permit free time during the busy holiday season.

At our house, Christmas was important. We lived for Christmas. I shopped for gifts throughout the year. Baking began after Thanksgiving with pies, cookies, and breads and ended with hand-dipped chocolates. On Christmas Eve, the celebrations started with a buffet and the opening of one gift. On Christmas morning, we opened the remaining gifts and ate a family breakfast. Later in the day, we celebrated again, dining on turkey and playing board games, which were accompanied by much laughter and raucous bickering about cheating.

Later that week, my husband, Bob, and I gloomily discussed the options of a tree, decorations, cookies, pies, turkey, buffet, and gifts. We decided that this year—the first year since our children had been born—we would forgo the trappings of the holidays and eat dinner out.

Bob suddenly looked old. Occasionally he sighed and then stared into space. As the weeks passed, I found myself devoid of my usual holiday spirit. Depressed, I felt as though I had lost someone dear. After all, we are told that Christmas isn't Christmas without family. Magazines smother us with words of family gatherings. Television shows depict the joy of loved ones together for the holidays. But this year we would have no one. No one. We had lost Christmas!

One day in early December our daughter called. "So Mom, what are you doing? Have you got the freezer filled with goodies yet?"

Sadly, I told her our plans.

"What did you and Dad do for the holidays before we were born?" she asked.

It was then that I remembered those early years—newly married, with no money, and living two thousand miles from family. Suddenly, I was excited! Why couldn't we have a merry day without our children? After all, we could call them. I could still make candy and cookies and mail them off—a touch of home for them. I knew this holiday season would be more difficult for them than it was for us. My selfish thoughts dissolved as I rummaged in the closet for the cookie tins.

Bob whistled as he dug out the Christmas lights and outlined the house with color. Soon the fragrance of cinnamon and nutmeg filled our home. We surrounded the crèche with pine boughs from the tree in our garden.

Christmas Eve arrived and Bob and I ate from our buffet. We opened one gift, sat before the fire, and listened to Bing Crosby Christmas albums.

At Midnight Mass, the young priest stood before an altar resplendent in red poinsettias and pine boughs, and his words touched my heart. "Do not be afraid, for behold, I bring good news of great joy which shall be to all the people . . ."

On Christmas morning, we opened our gifts and prepared the turkey. At dusk, peace surrounded us as we walked hand-in-hand across the lawn and watched as stars began to glow. Colorful lights brightened the neighborhood. A soft breeze hummed through the fir trees. Smoke from the neighborhood fireplaces blanketed the air with the smell of comfort.

We hadn't lost Christmas after all. It had always been there, waiting for us in that silent holy night.

LOIS ERISEY POOLE

CULTURE CLASH

When I think of cultural differences, I used to think of people in foreign lands. But I've learned that there are plenty of cultural differences right here at home. I don't have to leave the country to find people who live a life that's foreign to me. In fact, after a few years of marriage to a "foreigner," I've found I don't even have to leave the state! Sometimes diversity is, literally, only miles away.

My husband grew up in rural northern Illinois, while I grew up in a *Wonder Years*–like suburb seventy miles east of his family farm. We technically both come from the same generation, but he had just graduated from high school as I was finishing fifth grade.

The first indication that we had a "culture clash" was when we were planning our wedding reception. He said a cash bar was the norm in the area—I thought making our guests pay for their drinks would be tacky. The solution? We supplied champagne, soda, coffee, and tea, eliminating any kind of bar at all. In this instance, we compromised and were both relatively happy with the outcome. But this was just the beginning of the cultural chasm between us.

My husband has coined the phrase "Out here in the country . . ." to describe his rituals as opposed to my traditions. "Out here in the country" families don't sleep past 6:00 A.M. any day of the week. Breakfast, lunch, and supper are the three meals of the day. Teen social lives revolve around family, school, and church. "Where everybody knows your name" is not just a tag line from an old TV show's theme song. The television is not turned on unless it's the dead of winter and there is absolutely nothing else to do. A tree from the local tree farm is a must at Christmas. There are no hot dogs in chicken noodle soup. And Santa Claus leaves presents unwrapped under the tree.

Now, in reality (or at least the reality of my past), weekends are for sleeping late. You serve breakfast, lunch, and dinner (I really have no clue exactly what supper is). If you're a teen or young adult, your social life revolves around school, but you really don't acknowledge your family or church as part of your realm of existence unless you're forced to. You may know your neighbor's name if you're really nosy. The TV is an icon that deserves to be viewed at least three hours a day. Artificial trees are much easier to deal with than real ones. There are always hot dogs in chicken noodle soup (although I have come to realize that this is a Bavarian tradition of my mother's, not a suburban rite of eating). And Jolly Old Saint Nick would rather die than put anything but a nicely wrapped gift under a tree.

When my husband and I met and decided to marry, it was pretty much a given that we would live in the country. My husband had been born and raised there. He and his brother own the family farm, so he had responsibilities as well.

I wasn't exactly pleased about living someplace that, to me, might as well have been the end of the earth. I even wondered if I was up to the challenge. After all, I was used to having a mall at my fingertips—just a few minutes away in any direction—and a fast food establishment on every corner. I had not been raised on a farm. I have vague recollections of a farm that was owned by friends of my grandmother's, but it was a place to run and play for an afternoon, not a way of life. Besides, their big black Labrador lived outside. Who in their right mind would relegate something as wonderful as the family dog to the outdoors twenty-four hours a day?

Despite my suburban upbringing—or perhaps because of it—I have adapted to some things "out here in the country." I love getting up early on weekends and getting a head start on the day. I relish not having neighbors right next door and the fact that my kids can play in the woods half a mile away and still be in their own backyard. Picking out a real Christmas tree has become a beloved annual tradition for my family. I enjoy knowing just about everyone I see at the local grocery store. And our dog, and numerous cats, live outdoors year-round and are none the worse for wear.

But the fact remains that I eat dinner, not supper, television is still an important leisure activity, and I will always adore hot dogs in my chicken noodle soup. My husband, on the other hand, will always eat supper, doesn't watch much television, wouldn't put a hot dog in his soup if you paid him, and is of the persuasion that Mrs. Claus doesn't need to hit the after-Christmas sales for wrapping paper because Mr. Claus doesn't use it.

We've learned to accept and even celebrate each other's differences and, somewhere along the way, have even found things in common despite our very different upbringings. I will listen to my husband talk about combines and corn futures and even find it interesting once in a while. When I want to curl up in a chair with the latest Stephen King bestseller or make a trip to the mall, he lovingly obliges me with the time to do so.

Not only have I risen to the occasion of country living, but also there's no obliging one another now when we fire up the barbecue on a warm summer evening. The smell of fresh-cut hay hangs in the air. We sit in our big backyard, enjoy a glass of iced tea with our meal, comment on the beautiful sunset, and agree that—at times like these—we're definitely on common ground.

MICHELLE PEARSON

III
LASTING LEGACIES

Nobody has ever measured, not even poets,

how much the heart can hold.

ZELDA FITZGERALD

THE ANNIVERSARY CARD

I heard about couples who loved one another so deeply that they could almost read each other's thoughts. As a girl I dreamed of this sort of closeness, as a woman I found it with the man I married. We had an unspoken language, a knowing, about each other. He said the words I was about to say. He called me as I was calling him. We even had many of the same dreams at night. We knew we had a special gift, and we cherished it. However, as our seventh anniversary approached, our relationship began to change, and we felt a distance grow between us.

In one aspect, the distance was literal. We were rarely in the same place at the same time. My husband left before dawn each morning, traveled an hour to his job, worked his scheduled eight-and-a-half-hour shift, and then drove an hour back home. We would exchange a quick kiss at the door as I exited for my full-time night position. We knew our children were benefiting by this arrangement, but our marriage was suffering.

We talked on the phone every day, but the conversations became scripted and forced.

"How was your drive in?" I asked.

"Okay. The usual."

"Was there much traffic?"

"Not too bad. How was your night?"

"Fine. Nothing special. What do you want for dinner tonight?"

"It doesn't matter, whatever you want."

We continued the small talk until someone at work needed him or the kids needed me.

I missed the discussions we used to have. We no longer talked of news and politics—the only current event I knew was the *Sesame Street* letter of the day. We didn't talk about his work because the boss was within earshot. We didn't discuss books or movies because it was months since I had enjoyed either.

We were together on weekends, but despite the proximity we rarely said the things we needed to say. The stresses of the week made us tired and irritable, and the majority of our time was spent arguing.

In addition to the physical distance, we also seemed to be growing apart emotionally. Saying "I love you" became habitual instead of meaningful. We didn't have time to bare our souls or share our dreams. We were too busy and too tired to work on improving our relationship. We became little more than two people sharing a life.

This emotional distance grew with my increasing resentment of our situation. I woke with the children at seven in the morning, spent the entire day caring for them and the house, then went to work at a mind-numbing job until three the following morning. I envied the fact that my husband got to have time for himself each evening after putting the kids to bed. I was jealous that he could watch TV, read books, and sleep. I was ashamed of how I felt, so I never let him know. This silent suffering made the problem even worse.

I became very depressed as I noticed our anniversary approaching. I had read that the seventh year is the hardest: *This is the year where people experience the "Seven Year Itch" and become unfaithful. The seventh year is often a turning point in a relationship where previously minor annoyances become intolerable. A disproportionate number of couples divorce during their seventh year of marriage.* Out of fear I believed these myths, and attributed our strains to these fallacies.

The day before our anniversary, I dragged myself to the card shop to search for the perfect sentiment. After all, I convinced myself, this might be the last anniversary card I would give him. As I read through piece after piece, my eyes burned with tears. I was so in love and so afraid of losing the man who meant the world to me. I realized that I needed to let him know how I felt so I could get past the pain and fear. I needed to work on returning our relationship to the way it had been. I needed to remember how deeply we were connected.

After an hour of reading, I found the perfect card. One that said everything I was feeling. It was as if I had written it myself. It spoke of the love and commitment of marriage. It reminded lovers to share hopes and dreams, setbacks and disappointments. It challenged couples to reinvest in their relationships to make every day as magical as the day the anniversary celebrates.

I slipped the card in his briefcase on the morning of our anniversary; then went to sleep.

When I woke, I went downstairs to find an envelope that was addressed to me on the kitchen table. As I opened the flap, I saw the familiar artwork of the card I had given him. The words were still fresh in my mind. We had bought the same card for each other. As I grabbed the phone to call him, it began to ring.

"Hello?" I said.

His answer, "I love you so much."

"I love you, honey," the words came, choked by tears.

"I'm leaving work now, so we can spend the day together. Will you call off tonight?"

"As soon as we hang up."

"I'll see you in an hour, then."

"I can't wait."

Suddenly the distance narrowed. When he arrived home we talked and laughed and enjoyed each other's company in a way we hadn't in a long while.

Maybe the stars had correctly aligned. Maybe there was Divine intervention. Or, perhaps it is true that some lovers really can read each other's thoughts.

LISA SANDERS

A baby is God's way of saying the world should go on.
AUTHOR UNKNOWN

A NEW DAWN

*L*ast September my daughter, Laura, gave birth to her second child, Aaron. His birth brought back memories of Laura telling me the first time that she would be a mother, and I, a grandmother. I cried happy tears. But deep within, something else stirred.

Four years earlier, my seventeen-year-old daughter, Dawn, had died after an automobile accident. Her death was an event that cast me into a role for which I had never auditioned—grieving mother.

A few years before her death, when a similar tragedy had occurred within our community, Dawn had expressed sadness that a parent ever could lose a child. I had known I would never survive the death of a child of mine. Surely I would die, too, unable to bear the pain. And at the time of Dawn's unnatural death, I did want to die, longed to die, imagined ways to die, but thoughts of my other children kept me attached by a narrow thread, guiding me through my haze of sorrow.

Now a new person would be born into our family. I remembered a dream that had occurred some months after Dawn's death.

In my sleeping mind's eye, I had seen Dawn sitting in a serene place surrounded by endless numbers of babies spread about like wild field daisies. She was joyous beyond description. The dream left me a gift of peace. With the news of the impending birth came a gift of promise restored, for so much had remained unfulfilled when Dawn's life ended.

But when Laura informed me that if the baby were a girl, she would be named in memory of her sister, I found myself wondering, *Had I known this? Why didn't I know this? I should have known this, without being told.*

I had tried to respond with pleasure, but it was feigned because my mind was busy trying to process the news through a growing sense of panic. *Wait,* I wanted to say, *that was my little girl's name. Don't you understand? How can I look into the eyes of a baby girl, call her Dawn Michelle, and not weep at the very speaking of the name?* Against my better intentions, I struggled with the idea.

An early spring telephone call sent me rushing to the hospital, but the rush was unnecessary—the clock on the wall ticked on. This child would take a day and a night and another morning to be born. Tired, I muttered encouraging words, wiped Laura's brow, and massaged her swollen ankles. Her husband, Ron, and I coached from opposite sides of the bed. The hours passed the twenty-four mark. We watched Laura, exhausted and carefully monitored, run her marathon. Determined to cross the finish line, to succeed at natural childbirth, she knew surgeons now waited outside the door.

Wearied by the emotion-filled hours, my son-in-law gave in to worry and tears rolled from his eyes. Barely holding back my own, I looked across the bed at Ron and promised him, "She's strong. She'll be OK."

Into a room filled with exclamations of delighted relief, the baby was finally born. The midwife placed a healthy, rosy bundle of baby girl across Laura's chest. Wrapping her arms around her daughter, Laura quivered with exhaustion, wisps of hair sticking to her face.

Wrapping an arm around Laura's shoulders, I bent to kiss her. Looking into each other's eyes, we wept. Sweet tears of joy, mingled with a hint of sadness.

But it was all right. For here was a new Dawn. As I smiled down at my daughter and hers, life seemed to whisper gently in my ear, *See, aren't you glad you stayed?*

BEVERLY FROEHLICH

Tenderness is greater proof of love than the most passionate of vows.
MARLENE DIETRICH

LETTING GO SOFTLY

A young couple poses for formal portraits in the flower-filled grounds of her parents' home in France. She sits on a stone ledge in a bed of lavender wearing a cotton-lace wedding gown; he, in an elegant tuxedo, bends protectively over her. Later the wedding cortege winds through narrow streets to an ancient church as villagers lean from their windows applauding and bells peal approval. A six-year-old in a flowered frock, front tooth missing, a wreath of summer flowers slipping from her hair, solemnly elevates a ribboned pillow with the wedding rings.

That evening the celebration continues in a rustic stone restaurant—champagne; a multicourse meal; dancing; dignified grandmothers dressed in black reigning in one corner, tapping their canes to the music. A week later there's an evening reception in a Houston skyscraper—harpist and band, more good food, wine, and dancing, as American friends meet the bride and her family and bless the union.

The marriage of Brad, our eldest son, and Elisabeth, the Frenchwoman he met and wooed in graduate school in Arizona, began that August in a tiny French village on a day filled with sunshine, love, promise, and hope. It ended nearly five years later with a phone call from Brad in Tokyo, his voice filled with pain as he told us they were separating, and she was returning to France. Stunned, I cried, and my husband's voice stumbled as we said we were sorry, we loved them, and we'd help in any way we could. After we hung up, we tried to tell each other their marriage wasn't over, but Brad had seemed certain that it was.

Leaving New York for Tokyo had been hard for them. They had loved Manhattan—their brownstone apartment in Chelsea, long walks in Central Park on the weekend, lots of friends, challenging and fulfilling careers. When Brad was transferred, Elisabeth seemed positive about experiencing another culture, requested a job transfer there too, and immediately began to study Japanese. But we worried when she had to remain in New York for six months to train her replacement.

When we visited them in Tokyo, it was clear that despite her efforts to adapt and good will on both their parts, she was very un-happy. They fought during our stay, and we returned home wor-ried and anxious. Brad's sad phone call came eight months later. Separated for a year, they moved through the initial pain to ten-derness and friendship as they agreed to a "no-fault" divorce. The dissolution of their marriage was as amicable as parents who love them both could have wished. When Elisabeth returned to Tokyo to reclaim some joint property, Brad invited friends to a farewell party for her.

And yet I mourned for more than a year. I couldn't seem to stop the flow of memories or put away my dreams for them. I didn't want to divorce my first daughter-in-law. As the mother of three sons, I had been thrilled to welcome another woman into our family. When the boys were growing up, I embraced every girl they ever brought home—sporty girls who shot baskets in the driveway for hours, brainy girls who crammed for AP course exams and college-bowl quizzes, and girls with ribbons in their hair who sang like angels.

But when Elisabeth walked through our door for her first

"meet-the-parents" weekend, I gave my heart to this petite, bright, ambitious Frenchwoman with her charming accent, incredible blue-green eyes, and long dark braid flipped over one shoulder. The more I saw of her, the more I loved her. Practical, she taught me how to tie a scarf, how to choose a fish, and how to make a hollandaise that didn't curdle and a perfect apple tart. Diplomatic, she could sweetly cajole a houseful of men comfortable in their sweats into dressing for special family dinners.

Dedicated to her job, she once spent a night at the New York docks to be certain the cargo of an important client was properly loaded for shipping. Eager for an education, she had left her village at fourteen to live with a sister and attend high school in Lyon. No, I didn't want to divorce Elisabeth—daughter-in-law, adult friend, and daughter I never had.

I also didn't want to divorce her family. Although we had no common language with her parents, and we were not able to visit with them very often, we shared essential values, and our few times together were filled with laughter and love. When their son married, they included us as houseguests—as well as our second son, his wife, and her twin sister. Another summer, they welcomed our youngest son and his friend backpacking across Europe.

After the divorce, we would have liked to have called them when we heard that Elisabeth's grandmother had died. But Elisabeth had been our translator, so I sent a card and hoped her parents understood what I didn't write.

My friends told me divorce is worse when there are children. But I had dreamed of what a child of theirs would be like—a fortunate bilingual child blessed with loving grandparents on two continents. I grieved the loss of that child for whom I had already put away two gifts—a handmade yellow knit baby sweater my mother sent me when Brad and Elisabeth became engaged and a musical stuffed dog I once bought because it played "Frère Jacques."

But time moves on. Our second son and his wife, who had been living in Russia, her home, moved to Texas, and we are blessed to spend more time with them. Elisabeth married a Frenchman whom Brad likes very much. We stay in touch with her through phone calls and e-mail. When she told us last summer that she was pregnant, I wrapped up the musical dog and mailed it to her.

The baby sweater? I'm keeping that for the child our second son and his wife expect this fall.

SuzAnne C. Cole

DOWN FOR THE COUNT

Wrestling in the Vatican isn't usually advertised in travel brochures, but during the summer of 1962 a championship match took place inside St. Peter's Basilica.

I was traveling with my parents on a once-in-a-lifetime trip to Italy. My mother, a devout Catholic, insisted we visit the Vatican in the hopes of getting the pope's blessing. I thought it was a marvelous idea. Of course, at nine years old, I thought everything my mother suggested was a good idea. My father and brother were less enthusiastic.

We rented rooms at a convent adjacent to the Vatican City for convenience's sake. Our spartan rooms with spit-shined floors were decorated with crucifixes and pictures of saints, not the lace curtains and bowls of fresh fruit by the night stand that we might've enjoyed at some charming old pensione. What was my mother thinking?

The nuns did, however, gladly arrange our tour of the Vatican for the following day, and it occurred to me that perhaps my mother was on to something. Staying at the convent *had* to be an automatic "in" with His Holiness. I imagined a private audience in a red velvet parlor where my family would receive the papal blessing, ferret out a few shortcuts to paradise, and then all celebrate the moment together with lemon gelati. I couldn't wait.

Preblessing preparation was no simple matter. It involved meticulous grooming and passing my mother's careful inspection from gum line to anklets. She even spit on her hankie and wiped off a speck of scrambled egg that was stuck to my cheek from breakfast. My brother, Florio, older and wiser, ducked out of sight and avoided having his cowlicks tamed by the revolting "saliva" styling-gel technique. Preened, polished, and spiritually pumped, we left the convent and followed our tour guide to St. Peter's.

Reality hit hard as we were herded into a huge visitation hall with several hundred other people from all over the world. No private parlor—no gelato—and no cozy chat with the big guy.

As the official visitation time drew closer the audience swelled and elbowroom was only a memory. It was stuffy and hot and my air supply seemed to be dwindling rapidly. From my vantage point the only things visible were love handles, backsides, and a few hairy European armpits. I looked to my mother for reassurance and saw her hands delicately pressed together and eyes closed in prayer. I tried to do the same but my arms were pinned to my body. She looked down at me and returned a saintly smile that told me in a few minutes it would all be worth it.

Two hours later, His Holiness began making his way through the adoring crowd, reaching his hand out to be kissed by those lucky few. My mother whispered that he was coming toward us. Anticipation heightened. I wanted to see him, touch him, let him know that I wore my pink organza frock and patent leather shoes just for him.

Suddenly I felt myself moving effortlessly forward without the use of my legs. Could it be a miracle, I wondered? Were the angels lifting me? No, it was the crush of the crowd moving en masse, carrying me in its current. I felt myself being pulled away from my mother—swallowed whole by the hungry crowd—and a twinge of panic set in.

Then without warning a brawny woman who looked like Heidi on steroids began yelling at me in German for getting in front of her. She nudged me aside with forearms twice the size of my father's and continued to hurl a stream of guttural sounds from deep within her throat. I'd heard my grandfather make similar sounds in the bathroom once when he was trying to dislodge phlegm.

I desperately searched a sea of faces for my mother, but all I saw was a Rottweiler with braids. I began to wail. Forget the pope—I wanted my mother!

Suddenly and out of nowhere she appeared to rescue me as only mothers of crying children could do. The next thing I recall was seeing long blond braids flash before my face and the woman attached to them crash to the floor. My mother (all 120 pounds of her) kneeled over the woman, pinned her to the ground, and threatened to make Wiener schnitzel out of her if she touched me again. Heidi surrendered quickly and my mother stood triumphant, her pious demeanor replaced with noble indignation.

I dare say the pope lost a small portion of his audience's attention during Mom's scuffle and she missed seeing him altogether. Later, when I told her I was sorry, she confided, "Don't worry, sweetie; before we left I dipped my fingers in the holy water and licked them . . . doesn't get any better than that!"

That night we didn't return to the convent but stayed at a cozy hotel. I assumed the nuns got word of the rumble and, well, it wasn't too hard to figure out the rest. Who cared? The matronly innkeeper with rosy cheeks and colossal breasts welcomed us with open arms and a box of chocolates, and already I'd forgotten about being escorted out of the church by security guards. And except for the very serious mustache above her lip (which caused both my twelve-year-old brother and my fifty-three-year-old father to question their testosterone levels), I thought she was perfect. Warm, loving, jovial . . . and a mother of six.

The Vatican "incident" was certainly not a life-or-death situation, but nonetheless, my mother courageously protected me as though it was. I was proud of her. Still am. And when I became a mother I was able to understand the depth of her love and the ferocity of maternal instinct.

I admit I still get claustrophobic in large crowds. And ask me to wait in line for more than a few minutes? Forget it. However, what I will do is defend the right of any mother to protect her child from harm—and get the heck out of her way, if she's already in the process.

CAROL F. FANTELLI

There will be stars over the place forever.
SARA TEASDALE

KEEP IT IF YOU CAN

As we walked in the door from Ben's funeral the phone was ringing. Calling was my real estate agent in Vermont wondering if we would like to rent or sell our vacation house. They hadn't known that Ben died of cancer three days before.

One of the last discussions we had was about our Vermont house. "Keep it if you can," Ben whispered laboriously, as he bravely dictated his wishes to me two days before dying at age forty-three. I couldn't believe he thought I would be capable of continuing without him. Never mind keeping the house in Vermont and continuing our family skiing tradition, with two young children to raise. But I promised him that I would.

About two and a half years ago, three months before Ben's diagnosis, we purchased a vacation house in Vermont. We were young, had two children and a lifetime of happiness ahead of us. The house was not perfect; it certainly needed some work, but Ben was very handy and would like nothing better than fixing up this house with Jared, our ten-year-old son.

Ben couldn't wait to teach Lara, age six, how to ski—just as he had with Jared. So much to look forward to.

It was a rainy afternoon the day the three of us packed up and headed north for our first attempt to ski without Ben. I was nervous about arriving at the house in the dark. This trip would be difficult in many ways because I knew our emotions were running high. Little did I know what challenges the next few days would hold.

The two-and-a-half-hour trip turned into a five-hour ride on black ice, so we arrived late and hungry and our bladders were full. To our surprise, there were three dead mice in our toilet. I could hear Ben whispering in the back of my mind, "Never flush a mouse down the toilet in Vermont." Never mind three. Too scared to remove the mice, we relieved ourselves outside in the snow. Oh, I could hear Ben laughing at us now! A flat tire and an empty oil burner added to our adventure.

After finally enjoying a nice dinner at Brickers Restaurant, our family favorite, we shared some wonderful yet painful memories of happier days in Vermont with Ben. How he loved the snow and mountains and how the house was always filled with laughter. We also remembered how courageous Ben was in his fight against cancer. He showed his family and friends the way to fight this disease with faith and hope. Even in his daily battle with chemotherapy and radiation, he always believed that tomorrow would be a brighter day. He taught us to hold on tight to hope and to the people and the places that mean most to us.

It started to snow. It warmed our hearts because the last time we had seen snow was the day Ben died. We knew we would feel a strong connection to him on this trip, since this was the place that held our dreams.

When we entered the house there were reminders of him all around. Notes he had jotted down, books he had left here to read, unfinished projects. It reminded us that Ben would want us to go on with life, to be happy, especially in Vermont. It would be hard, yet we couldn't help but smile.

The next day the three of us attempted skiing at Okemo Mountain. Ben had never seen Lara ski, or even ride a chair lift, and I was determined that she would do this. He would be so happy and proud of us. How sad that he wouldn't see this and so many of his dreams and plans for his little family he loved so much.

When we finally got to the top of that mountain I was physically and emotionally exhausted, but I felt an enormous relief. Somehow on this day the view was a thousand times lovelier than I had remembered. I could feel Ben's presence, gentle and warm, silent in the snow. I hugged the kids. We were happy. We had made it! Overwhelmed, I tried to fight back the tears.

Wearing Ben's ski jacket because it was warm and extra large on me, I could stuff the pockets with anything the kids might need on the ski slope. Reaching into an inside pocket for a tissue, I pulled out a three-by-five card Ben must have used the last time he wore the coat. He was famous for making lists and writing notes and quotes on these cards. This one read, "VT—keep if you can." My heart was pounding. I clutched the card. Excitement overcame me. Ben *was* near—here on this mountaintop. He was with us, showing us the way, and he was happy that we tried. We could feel his pride and see his bright smile at this unforgettable moment. It was magical, the four of us on top of that mountain. We were comforted knowing that Ben was leading us and loving us through it all.

With an understanding that everything would be all right, we felt protected by a warm blanket of peace. Our tears were of joy and of hope for the future. And with love and happiness in our hearts, we slowly skied down that mountain knowing that we would keep the Vermont house and Ben would remain with us forever.

DIANE NOVINSKI

SNAKE PLANTS

For as long as I can remember my mother grew snake plants. Dishes of tall, green variegated spires lined the extended windowsill in the foyer of our Brooklyn apartment. The swordlike plants were the first sights you beheld as you walked through the doorway. She tended those plants almost as carefully as she did her family, my father, and me.

I never understood why she seemed to like those stiff, unattractive towers of vegetation. To me they displayed no sensuality, no charm, and certainly no beauty to be featured in a prominent location in our residence. But, through my mother's constant nurturing, the number of plants, containers, and allocated space for them increased from year to year.

The original plant, or the mother plant, had been given to her as a gift in the hospital after she gave birth to me, my mother frequently told me. It was like a miniature Japanese garden with tiny bridges, pagodas, and a variety of plants all landscaped in a shallow, square, jade-colored container. While there were several different varieties of plants to begin with, the only one to survive into my childhood, and later, into my care when my mother died, was the snake plant. From that one plant came the cuttings that she had placed into numerous dishes and flowerpots in our apartment.

I always knew that I was a child who was truly wanted by my parents. My mother and father were forever retelling how it took years for my mother to get pregnant. It was eight and a half years after they were married that I was born. I had heard the same story many times about how my mother finally found the great Dr. Shapiro, who treated her and helped her conceive and deliver a child. Mother's pregnancy and delivery were difficult. She had toxemia, and I was born with the umbilical cord wrapped around my neck.

Maybe it was the significance of the gifts, childbirth and plant, that kept that snake plant so important in her life. Maybe it was her loving nature that made her want to nurture and care for a living thing. For whatever reason, I took over caring for the plants after she died.

Fifteen years after my mother's death, I learned that I was pregnant, and my husband and I were thrilled that we were to have a child. Before I could revel in the news of my pregnancy, I had to be rushed to the hospital because I was hemorrhaging. My obstetrician provided excellent care. He gave me hope that the fetus would survive, and that I would have a baby at the end of the pregnancy.

Upon my return from the hospital, my father died suddenly in Florida. Because of my condition, I could not attend the funeral of the father I loved so much. There would be one more emergency run to the hospital for hemorrhaging and five months in bed before the premature birth of my healthy, beautiful baby girl.

It was upon my return from the first stay at the hospital that colleagues at my office sent me a get-well plant. It was a miniature Japanese garden planted in a dark-green, round bowl with four different varieties of plants, one being a snake plant. For the last thirty years I have tended and cared for that potted plant. Two of the four plants died, but the philodendron and snake plant survived. I still don't like snake plants, and I am not increasing the hoard by making cuttings from the original plant. But as it was for my mother, it's a way to express my gratitude for having a daughter born to me.

MARILYN BURKHARDT

The human contribution is the essential ingredient.
It is only in the giving of oneself to others that we truly live.
Ethel Percy Andrus

CHARITY BEGINS AT HOME

When my daughters came home a couple of weeks ago and asked if they could have some food from the cupboards for their school's canned-food drive, I said no. It's not that I'm heartless; I just don't see the value—for the recipients or for my kids—if we donate a few cans that have been shoved to the back of the shelf. Call me crazy, but I just don't feel comfortable donating garbanzo beans and tomato paste to people who are hungry.

I told my kids to decide how much of their own money they were each willing to contribute, and that I would match them dollar for dollar. Then we would go out and buy the most nutritious canned foods available. I hoped they would learn that giving isn't merely an afterthought, but sometimes requires effort and sacrifice.

Fortunately, Alex, my second-grader, is studying the food pyramid. When we go grocery shopping, she says cute things like, "Mom, I see you have a lot of things in your cart that are from the top of the pyramid. You need to even that out." This amuses our fellow shoppers and sometimes embarrasses me. When she had to write a composition about her favorite things, the Grains Group made the list, alongside the Rugrats and her cat, Eddie. So when we sat down to plan for the food drive, I asked my little nutritionist to lead the discussion.

First, we had to decide how much to spend. One daughter pledged ten dollars, the other offered three, and I matched their contributions. Then, we had to decide what to buy. Alex gave us a quick lesson on the food pyramid before recommending that we choose items from the meat group. Mackenzie, my nine-year-old, added that soup would be an excellent second choice. Armed with twenty-six dollars and our good intentions, we went to the Canned Food Outlet since it's close to our house and, as Mackenzie pointed out, they have canned food there.

This turned out to be not only a lesson about giving, but also a primer on math and budgeting. We compared prices and quantities and figured out exactly how much tuna twenty-six dollars would buy. We did the same thing with various kinds of soup. From time to time, one child or the other would come up with another idea, like sardines or asparagus. I reminded them several times that we had only twenty-six dollars to spend and therefore needed to make thoughtful, responsible choices.

It never occurred to me that other people might have noticed us. I hadn't really paid attention to anyone else in the store, although there were a few shoppers here and there. Just as we had decided to buy twenty-six dollars worth of tuna, which worked out to 104 cans, a man who was pushing his cart in our direction asked if I knew where the canned fruits were. I pointed to the next aisle over. As he walked past, he stepped very close to me and pressed a piece of paper into my hand and said, "Please don't say no." His voice cracked a bit, as though he were holding back tears. "Please, just do not say anything." He was talking loudly, apparently trying to drown out any objections I might raise, although I had no idea what he didn't want me to object to.

Bewildered to say the least, I opened my hand and saw part of Andrew Jackson's face. He had given me twenty dollars, and for no discernible reason. I turned around to say something to him, but as he rounded the corner, he was still talking. He said, "Sometimes God just tells you to do things," as he disappeared into the next aisle.

Mackenzie and Alex were counting tuna cans, oblivious to what had just taken place. I stood there trying to figure out how this man knew we were buying for charity.

He didn't know. He couldn't have known.

Suddenly, I realized how we must have looked to people wandering past. The kids were suggesting things, and I kept telling them we had only twenty-six dollars to spend. Alex had suggested boxed macaroni and cheese, and I had reminded her that milk and butter are needed to mix with it, so maybe it wasn't such a good idea. I had dismissed canned ham as too expensive. I had endorsed tuna because of its high protein and low price.

He thought I was spending my last nickel to feed my family.

I started to go after him to object, to tell him he'd made a mistake, that we aren't poor. That fortunately, I can feed my kids without any real worries. That I have a decent job with good pay and benefits, a place to live, a dependable car, three nice orange cats, and a big black dog. In truth, I wanted to return the money, not because I didn't need it or because I'm pure of heart, but because I didn't want him to think I was poor. As I pushed the cart through the store trying to spot the man, I wondered what I was going to say when I found him.

There wasn't a thing I could say. Was I going to tell him he'd made a mistake, that God hadn't told him to slip me a twenty at all?

Then, it hit me. I'm a bit slow sometimes. I was in the store teaching my kids a lesson about giving. A man walked up and gave me twenty dollars. It was not a mistake.

While I pushed the cart back to the tuna aisle, I explained to the kids that a nice man in the store had given us twenty dollars to buy more for the food drive. They excitedly piled eighty more cans of tuna into our cart.

In retrospect, it really doesn't matter that I was embarrassed because the man mistook me for something I'm not. What mattered is that when he perceived a need, he responded without hesitation. He didn't try to discern if I was a worthy recipient or if I would use it wisely; it didn't matter. It only mattered that he felt moved to give.

I still believe the lesson I wanted to teach my daughters that giving sometimes requires effort and sacrifice was correct—it just wasn't complete. I was only showing them one side of the coin. It's true that tuna makes a better meal than tomato paste. It's true that *giving* sometimes requires effort and sacrifice. What I neglected to add to the equation is that *receiving* may be the most difficult part of charity of all.

LISA WEST

AUNTIE'S ANTICS

My Auntie was possibly the most annoying person you could ever meet, with a gravelly voice that affected people like a fingernail scraping across a blackboard. When holding a conversation with Auntie, you were required to follow certain rules: Pay close attention at all times; don't interrupt; don't ask her to repeat herself; and never, ever, disagree.

When I was a child I was scared to death of her and later learned that most children were. Her voice was deep and loud and, as she proudly put it, "could carry further than anyone else's in the family."

Auntie lived in Portland, Oregon, and we drove from our home in Northern California to visit her almost every summer, something that I feared and dreaded. I never understood why we had to do this. My mother, Auntie's sister, tried to convince me that Auntie had a sweet side to her, but I didn't buy it. Perhaps it was Auntie's desire to be thought of as sweet that prompted her to contact all her nieces and nephews one year, demanding from that day forward that we refer to her as "Auntie Honey."

As I grew older, I realized she had some very nice qualities and could, on occasion, be very sweet. However, to the end, "Auntie Honey" remained a demanding and bossy woman. Auntie was the last of her generation in our family and loved to declare, "I will rule with a firm hand."

During our annual visits, we toured her home and beloved rose garden, followed by a quiz. It was required that all visitors notice any and all changes made during the previous year. God help you if anything new went unnoticed or if you innocently admired the new couch she had owned for years. A severe tongue-lashing would surely follow. These house inspections were not only painful, but also lengthy, for Auntie was a collector.

She collected roses, teapots, antiques, silver, crystal, and priceless porcelains. The rooms were filled with Waterford, Lenox, and Lladró. You name it, she collected it. Once a year the announcement was made to all her family and friends. "This year I am collecting crystal (or teapots or silver)." We then knew what we would be buying for her birthday and at Christmas that year.

Once, I forgot her birthday and called to apologize. "You have known for a year that it was coming," Auntie responded. After I had groveled in shame, she added, "Now, how are you? Do you need any money?" And she ended, as always, with, "I love you."

When I was a young mother, I flew north with my two little boys to visit Auntie. It was a command performance. My dear mother had passed on some months before, and Auntie felt that I needed to be with family. During that visit, she insisted I leave for a quiet afternoon alone and go shopping. As I backed her Dodge out of the drive, I could hear my youngest son screaming at the top of his three-year-old lungs.

I immediately reparked the car and rushed to his rescue. Auntie met me at the door. "You get right back into that car. Don't you dare come in." Her bellow was as loud and frightening as always.

"I can't leave," I insisted.

"Yes, you can. I have been caring for children for over forty years and have not yet met one I couldn't handle. Remember, I am bigger than he is."

Since she had then shut the door in my face, I drove to the mall and after listlessly wandering in and out of various shops for a slow couple of hours, I returned to the house. As I opened the door, instead of hearing the expected screams, I was treated to peals of laughter. I will never forget the sight that awaited me as I entered the living room. There were Auntie and my babies, sitting in a circle with a green felt cloth between them. Scattered around the floor were enough playing cards and chips to supply a small card room. Auntie was teaching my three- and four-year-old sons the fine art of playing poker.

It was then that I began to understand her gutsy child-rearing methods. She handled children like a military drill instructor. First she scared them half to death and then followed with sweetness. It proved to be effective because over the years Auntie helped raise many nieces, nephews, their children, and their grandchildren. It was because of her help that more than one youngster was able to complete his education.

As time passed, the traveling roles reversed. Each summer Auntie would fly to visit me in California, and each visit felt like the longest seven days of my life. Attempting to provide the required entertainment, I took her out to dinner almost every night. Auntie enjoyed fine dining, so by the time she departed I was always flat broke. The dinners themselves were agonizing for me because Auntie loved to steal. If it was on the table, it was fair game. Into her rather large handbag would disappear silverware, ashtrays, plates, glasses, cups, salt and pepper shakers, and on one occasion, a vase still full of flowers.

During a few of those yearly visits, I was divorced and living alone, so more than one male friend was privileged to meet Auntie. It was only later that I was told of her threats to them. "If you hurt her, you will answer to me. I'll hunt you down." I was always embarrassed, but never surprised.

Many years passed before I fully realized how much Auntie had taught me. She fostered in me the love of beautiful things and how to care for them. She taught me patriotism by example, encouraging her own sons to answer their country's call when they were drafted. She showed me the joy of lending a helping hand to family and friends. When money was involved, Auntie taught me the importance of insisting on a timely repayment. By serving weekly in the local soup kitchen, she demonstrated the beauty in giving. Her devotion to helping her family and many friends was her finest quality and the one that filled the chapel with mourners and flowers at her funeral.

I was out of the country when Auntie died and unfortunately was not able to return in time to attend her funeral. I know she would have wanted me to be there. I was told that it was a grand affair, each detail carried out as her instructions had dictated.

It has been several years now and not a day goes by that I don't think of her. I miss her still. I have been told on more than one occasion that Auntie's spirit lives in me. I suppose there are some similarities. I love fine dining, enjoy my rose garden, and have a collection of crystal as well as many teapots.

If I should happen to be the last of my generation, I promise that I, too, will be the one to rule with a firm hand—and hopefully, pass that legacy on.

MAUREEN MARY ROSENBERG

DO GANG MEMBERS
EAT BANANAS?

After a wonderful family Thanksgiving visit, I boarded the Southwest Chief heading back to Los Angeles. We were barreling along from Albuquerque to Union Station and the train was filled with the smell of homemade turkey sandwiches and white bread. I had already overdosed on tryptophane that weekend, so I had declined my cousin's offer to make me my favorite—dark meat on rye, heavy on the mayo—to go.

Riding overnight in coach class on Amtrak is an experience. While the train has comfortable reclining seats and footrests, the intimacy level with strangers in the nonsleeperette section is heightened by the closeness of the seats. Experienced, economy-minded train riders wouldn't think of travelling without their basic needs for comfort. In addition to their suitcases, frequent Amtrak-ers often carry on shopping bags full of food, their full-size bed pillows, and a comfy king-size cotton quilt, in addition to their suitcases.

I was wearing my oldest, well-worn sweats with the loose, disintegrating elastic in the waistband and waiting to see who would be my travelling companion on the sold-out ride home. When we stopped to pick up additional passengers in Gallup, I shifted in my seat as the over-six-foot-tall, lanky young man with the black-and-pink spiked hair headed directly toward me. Oh God, I prayed, please don't do this to me. He was dripping in biker-black leather and silver chains, and I gulped when he asked to sit down for the almost thirteen-hour trip to L.A. When he took off his leather jacket and stripped down to his T-shirt, I tried to keep my eyes focused on his biceps, which were completely covered with tattoos, rather than stare at the painful-looking silver stud that pierced his skin just below his bottom lip.

There was absolutely no question in my mind—I was now seated next to the eighteen-year-old vacationing leader of the Crips or the Bloods gang, and I was going to spend the night sleeping next to him. In my paranoid state, I immediately dubbed him "Killer."

During our first hour together, I kept my nose buried in a stack of magazines I had carted along especially for the trip while Killer cranked up the volume on his Walkman. I usually love riding the train—for me it is like an oasis away from phone calls, e-mails, and responsibilities.

I was annoyed that Killer had come along to invade my space and disturb the peaceful end to my long weekend. The train lights were dimmed for the sleepy travelers, but I was wide awake when he reached under his seat and into his black nylon duffel bag. Surreptitiously peeking out of the corner of my eye, I watched and waited to see the Uzi or brass knuckles appear. Instead Killer pulled out a banana. Wrapped in my Mexican cotton blanket from home, I began to relax a little and wondered to myself, *Do gang members eat bananas?*

Killer ingested his potassium, didn't even acknowledge that I was alive, and we continued in silence for another two hours. I dozed off for a while and woke up when the train stopped in Flagstaff. By now, Killer was diving in for the second course of food from his goodie bag. I was starving and regretted having turned down my cousin's sandwich offer.

"Did you make that yourself?" I asked and wondered whether he would respond.

"No," he laughed affably, "my grandma made this stuff for me and she gave me a lot of extra food to take home."

We're making progress now, I thought. *Killer actually speaks.*

"Where's home?" I continued.

"Silver Lake, but I spent Thanksgiving with my mom, who lives outside of Gallup."

During the rest of the ride home, gentle, docile Killer shared half his sandwich with me and told me his name was Xavier. He was a member of a band and would be appearing in concert in an L.A. club in January. He told me he had grown up in California, but when his father left them when he was eleven, his mom packed up and moved the family back to Gallup. He has three sisters living in New Mexico and he's the only boy in the family. His grandparents helped raise all of them and his grandma is a great cook.

The trip and chatter were so pleasant that by the time we pulled into Union Station, I was ready to invite Xavier to Christmas Dinner. And if he came, I'd make his old family recipe that he told me all about on the train. It's called Grandma's Killer Turkey Quesadillas.

LINDA H. WATERMAN

IV
ANIMAL HOUSE

We are pretty sure that we and our pets share the same reality,

until one day we come home . . . and we shake our heads in

an inability to comprehend what went wrong here.

MERRILL MARKOE

My cat does not talk as respectfully to me as I do to her.
COLETTE

ANIMAL INTERVENTION

I was in the middle of a midlife crisis: I couldn't decide whether to resume my career as a dancer-singer in the professional theater or to return to college and finish my education.

One day, as a method of exploring my options, I decided to vocalize and brush up on my old audition songs. I sat down on my couch and happily began to sing show tunes. I let loose with "Summertime." Opposite me, lounging in her comfy chair, was my fluffy Persian kitten, Marilyn, whom I'd rescued from the animal shelter one week earlier.

I had been singing the same tune for about fifteen minutes when Marilyn jumped down from her chair, walked across the living room, jumped up on the couch, then up onto my lap, and put her paw across my mouth!

I got the message.

I stopped singing immediately and shortly thereafter registered for school.

FRANCINE M. STOREY

THE LOVE OF A DUCK

When my children were little, I bought a small farm and immediately began filling it with all sorts of animals. We always had a few dogs and cats around, mostly strays, and to those we added a couple of gentle old riding horses, some chickens, three goats, a lamb, and various other creatures.

One day I had the misfortune of falling in the barn and breaking my foot, which rendered me immobile for a few weeks. I was a miserable invalid and a lousy patient, constantly complaining about all the work that I needed to be doing. A dear friend decided to cheer me up by bringing me a newly hatched duckling. It was love at first sight. We didn't know what kind of duck it was, nor did I much care. I only knew that this fuzzy, funny little creature was the best remedy for depression anyone could have given me.

While I lay on the couch, Donald (what else would you call a duck?) had free range of my head, chest, and shoulders. His playful antics both amused and fascinated me. He would wander aimlessly around my chest, pecking here and there, inspecting the contents of a shirt pocket, or pulling on a button, or climbing up on my head to wander through my hair. He would peep happily away for a while, then grow sleepy and nuzzle in my armpit for a quick snooze. There is no doubt that Donald loved me as much as I loved him, and he remained a welcome houseguest for several weeks.

But the day came when I decided it was time for Donald to move to the barn with the rest of the animals. He was growing rapidly and definitely outgrowing my idea of a house pet. I carried Donald out to the barn, and laid him gently in a soft bed of straw. I filled his food and water dishes and sat down beside him, thinking I'd give him a chance to grow accustomed to his new surroundings. Donald refused to leave my lap, and I could see this move was going to be a much greater adjustment than I'd anticipated. The kittens came over for an inspection of the new tenant, but Donald was having none of it. I decided I'd just have to let him adjust on his own, so with one last pat of his downy feathers, I got up and firmly bid him farewell. "Quack, quack." Donald waddled right behind me, emitting a loud protest over my departure. The faster I moved, the faster he waddled, right out the barn door and back to the house.

Well, I thought, *he does think I'm his mother, after all, and it's natural for a duckling to stay with his mother.* I'd have to try another approach. I built a cozy little house for Donald, filled it with straw, and put it outside the kitchen door. Ducks are supposed to sleep at night, but Donald did nothing but quack for three nights straight. I felt as if I'd abandoned my child, but I knew that Donald had to adjust to outdoor life, so I remained steadfast. During the day, I'd take Donald back to the barn and stay with him. He gradually began to explore his surroundings, each day becoming more curious about the other animals. He especially liked the kittens, and they seemed to like him.

On the fourth night of our separation, I was relieved to notice the quacking had ceased. *Thank God,* I thought, *Donald is finally settling down.* I pictured him in his cozy little house outside the kitchen door, sleeping peacefully.

I awoke early the next morning, and hurried downstairs to check on Donald and assure him that I was still there. To my horror, the little house was empty. I quickly searched around the yard, but Donald was nowhere to be found. Although I'd waited until I felt Donald was mature enough not to be threatened by predators, I began to imagine the worst. I called for Donald everywhere, searching in bushes and behind trees. Finally, it occurred to me to look in the barn.

Yes, I'd left the barn door partially open, so perhaps he'd wandered in there. I opened the doors wide, exposing the dark interior to the early morning sun. One of the horses neighed, and the chickens began clucking for their morning feed, but there was no welcoming "quack, quack." I looked behind the hay bales, hoping he'd be sleeping in the bed I'd made for him a few days before, but the bed was empty. "Donald," I called, tears welling in my eyes. And then I heard him, a rather muffled quack coming from the other side of the barn. "Quack, quack." I followed the sound across the barn and toward the back. "Quack, quack." The sound was coming from the kittens' little house. I peered inside, and there was Donald, snuggled up with three kittens, thoroughly content, and not the least bit interested in coming out to say good morning.

My reaction to Donald's new independence was one of relief, but also tinged with a little sadness, rather like one feels on her child's first day of school. I knew our bond would never be quite the same, but I would always treasure the love that existed between two very different creatures. Ultimately, I was glad he'd finally made friends in the animal world, and I knew that we would always remain friends, too.

Donald matured into a magnificent mallard, befitting his name. He was very proud of his grand stature, and loved spreading his wings wide, letting the sunshine glisten on his beautifully colored feathers. He was, first and foremost, a grand duck, but he also displayed the playful qualities of a kitten. The kittens remained his best friends, and they grew into adulthood together.

One autumn morning, while working in the kitchen, I saw Donald waddling toward the house with great purpose, carrying something in his bill. "Quack, quack. Quack, quack." There was a definite urgency in his quacking. Curiosity peaked; I went to the kitchen door. "Quack, quack," said Donald proudly, flapping his wings excitedly. There, on the doorstep, was one neatly deposited dead mouse. "Thank you, my dear friend," I said quietly, a tear in my eye and a very broad smile on my face.

Years have passed, my children are grown with families of their own, and we now live on another farm, farther out in the country. But sometimes, when I drive into town, I pass our old property, and I smile, remembering my best friend, Donald.

NANCY TOMAZIC

CAT WARS

T*heir hissing takes me from deep sleep to sudden consciousness.* It isn't an unusual sound for this time of night in my home. Cat Wars have commenced in the bathroom adjacent to our bedroom. On some nights I sleep right through these battle cries. On other nights, they wake me.

The battlefield isn't always in the bathroom. Often it is in our family room on top of the couch. On occasion it's in one of our children's bedrooms. Sometimes it's in the kitchen. It all depends on where the cats decided to drop and snuggle in. There are nights when they snuggle under the blanket. There are nights when they end their day between our pillows. If UPS makes a delivery, bedtime often happens within the emptied carton.

Like human siblings, brother and sister cats have devoted their lives to antagonizing each other over the little details of their feline existence. Mostly it's about which cat has the better bed. I've sat and observed two content sleeping kitties become Cat Commandos from the Third Dimension in the matter of a split second over who has the better set of legs to snuggle against.

Tonight they're fighting over the sink. We have two sinks in our bathroom: My husband has claimed the one next to the medicine cabinet as his, and I have the other. The sinks are identical, although I am sure mine is cleaner. Each cat has taken a sink. Each cat has curled up in a ball and has snuggled in for the night. At least that's how I left them when I got into bed, turned off the light, and left the world behind me a few hours ago. Tonight Mr. Cat is in my sink and Mrs. Cat is in my husband's sink. When I left them to snuggle into the space where I end my day, all was fine in their feline world. They were purring in semiconsciousness, dreaming of bugs, mice, catnip, canned dinner, and a full water bowl.

But a few hours have passed, and I am brought to consciousness by the sound of hissing. I get out of bed to make sure they're not doing something questionable or potentially dangerous. It's a Mom thing.

I go into the bathroom and observe Mr. Cat standing over Mrs. Cat. He is swatting her on the head with his clawless paw. There is fear in each of his swats as Mrs. Cat hisses at her clawless, clueless brother, showing her teeth, and making it very clear that tonight she is sleeping in Daddy's sink, and she is definitely not in the mood to play this game. She has no intention of moving. She is bigger than her brother. I believe it's referred to as being large-boned, or maybe it's her need to satisfy her Inner Cat Woman by filling her stomach again and again and again with gourmet treats and table scraps.

I decide the cats are safe and I leave them to settle their own Cat Disputes. I've learned the hard way, with scars to prove it, that playing referee is a lesson in futility. As I am about to turn off the light in the bathroom, I notice Mr. Cat swat Mrs. Cat one more time. Mrs. Cat rises to her feet, arches her back, and chases Mr. Cat through my legs, out of the bathroom, and down the hallway to the children's bedrooms.

As I cuddle under the blankets, the cats re-enter the bedroom, leaping over the bed, one still in mad pursuit of the other. I can't see who is the chaser and who is the chasee, but I do hear my husband mumble something about how cats belong outdoors where God intended them and how good they'd look stuffed. I've also heard my husband on occasion threaten the cats that he was going to give them back to those nice people who placed the "Free to a Good Home" advertisement. I've heard him mutter, "This isn't a good home. I'll just ask for my money back." These cats were

"Free to a Good Home" almost a decade ago. I would hate to burst my husband's bubble by telling him that even if there had been a warranty, it has more than expired.

Tonight I just ignore him as the cats leap over the bed a second time. I pound my pillow to get the shape right and try to fall back to sleep on my side of the bed. I pull more than my share of the blanket to my side of the bed. It might be my imagination, but I think I hear my husband hiss.

FELICE R. PRAGER

Dog lovers are a good breed themselves.
GLADYS TABER

A BOUNTIFUL YEAR

"Pull over, Dan!" *I yelled to my husband as we raced along the* highway on our way to a family Thanksgiving celebration. I had just spotted a wet, too-thin dog standing on the shoulder of the freeway. He looked so sad, confused, and pathetic. This was not our first rescue; animals just seem to find us.

Dan quickly pulled off to the side of the road. Sheets of rain pelted me as I got out of the car. I crouched down as low as I could and called out to the frightened dog. Although wary, he cautiously stepped toward me. Underneath the dirt and grime, I could see that he was a young Australian shepherd.

My first concern was the black collar wrapped too tightly around his neck. No one had bothered to loosen it as he grew. The collar was so snug that it was difficult to remove. He was scared and nervous, but also very happy to see a friendly face. He wasn't wearing any tags, so we piled him into the backseat of our car. I joined him there, and he immediately pushed up against me as hard as he could and nuzzled his head behind mine. I stroked his trembling body, assuring him that everything would be fine. I told him that I would not let anything happen to him. That was our first encounter with the young dog we named Ozzie.

Almost immediately, we learned that Ozzie was an escape

artist. Because he was so dirty, we left him in the car while we ate Thanksgiving dinner. Oz managed to let himself out of the Jeep twice—even after we had locked it.

Once home, I bathed and combed Ozzie and discovered what a beautiful boy he was. As a blue merle Australian shepherd, Oz has tan eyebrows and tan flecks sprinkled throughout his long white and black hair. One eye is colored blue and the other eye is amber.

As we cared for Ozzie, we watched the newspaper ads every day to see if anyone was attempting to find a lost dog, but nothing appeared.

After living with Ozzie for a week, we made the gut-wrenching decision to look for a good home for Ozzie. We already had two other dogs, and we wondered whether three dogs and two cats were more than we could handle. Our grown daughter, Tawnie, thought her friend Brooke might be interested in Ozzie. We made an agreement that she would take him on a trial basis. The night before Ozzie was to go to Brooke's, I had a hard time sleeping and cried on and off during the night. I really felt a special bond with this dog, but I was also trying to be practical.

Ozzie had been with Brooke five days when she called to say that he had gotten out of her backyard and disappeared. Dan and I each took a car and drove to Brooke's house using different routes in hopes of finding Ozzie. Dan and Brooke made notices and posted them nearby, and I walked her neighborhood calling for Ozzie. I was afraid that we would never find him again, and I felt an overwhelming sense of loss and sadness.

That night I tossed and turned in bed. I finally got up in the middle of the night and walked around the house looking out the windows for a trace of Ozzie. I knew it was very unlikely that he would be able to make his way back to our house. I was tormented with not knowing where he had gone.

The next day, Dan headed straight for the county dog pound to see if Ozzie had been brought in. He showed a picture of Ozzie to the woman at the front desk. Excitedly, she said, "I believe we have that dog!" Dan walked back to the kennels with her and was overcome with emotion when he spotted Ozzie.

The records at the shelter showed that Ozzie had been picked up several blocks from our street. In his attempt to find his way back home, Ozzie had managed to head in a straight line—as the crow flies—in the direction of our house, and in the process, he walked six miles and crossed a multitude of some of Portland's busiest streets before Animal Control picked him up. He was coming home to his family.

We have always found good homes for the animals we've rescued, yet every now and then, we know that a particular animal is one we need to keep. Ozzie was one step ahead of us because he had already figured out where he belonged and that we were meant to be together. Brooke was more than gracious in allowing Ozzie to come home.

Ozzie has been with us almost a year now, and he has become an integral member of our family. He is a joyful, affectionate dog and is kind to everyone he meets. The perfect Mr. Oz no longer opens car doors. He knows right where he belongs and has no intention of leaving.

Four months ago, Oz and I were playing Frisbee in an open field near our home, and I came across a crate full of kittens abandoned in the tall grass with no food or water. I took the flea-bitten, starving felines home, and Dan and I nurtured them back to health. They all loved Ozzie. We kept two of them, and before we found good homes for the others, we'd often find a couple of dozing piles of kitties snuggled up next to Oz. It is my belief that animals that are rescued never forget what you've done for them. Just as he appreciates us, we cannot get enough of the Perfect Mr. Oz.

Our extended family has a tradition at Thanksgiving dinner where we go around the table and each of us says what we are grateful for. As "Turkey Day" approaches, I already know what

I'll say. Our family has grown in the most unexpected way and this has been a year of many blessings—one of the most significant being Ozzie.

CINDY POTTER

MAX

My daughter, at three, was endlessly curious. So, naturally, we had to stop and look in the shopping cart guarded by a large man standing in front of the big glass ShopRite doors. The small gray kitten opened one eye and looked at us, then resumed his meatloaf position in the carton in the bottom of the cart. Leery, concerned that our dog would feel betrayed if a new family member appeared unannounced, Jess pulled on my hand, but I was entranced. I asked the child to hold on to the kitten until I could buy the necessities, and twenty minutes later, Jess and Max and I were on our way home. Max, a lump of gray in Jess's lap, would inevitably rule our household from that throne.

It was a silent ride home. Both Jess and I had been distraught at the sudden move to a place we hadn't chosen. I was mourning a troubled marriage, and we were both grieving the passing of my mother. The sadness was almost overwhelming, but Max napped, unconcerned, and filled the car with the smell and sound of cat. He had the loudest purr I'd ever heard.

Max was to become the spearhead and king of the horde of animals that passed through our lives over the years. They soothed and comforted, annoyed and entertained, each in their own way, but none was like Max, into whose warmth we poured so much of ourselves. He came when we were at a low point and brought laughter where there was sadness and love where there was none. He became the focal point and the translator when we were too angry to deal with each other.

Time passed and days at our beach house became a distant memory as Max and Jess grew together and we settled uneasily into our new mountain home. At three she shrieked gleefully at his courageous assaults on the immense hind end of our collie. At four, she carried him slung over her shoulder, chattering to him as she went about her day. At seven she complained about his making footprints in her hair at night, but she and the restless sleeper eventually made their peace. At ten she dressed him in doll's clothing. At fourteen he kept her company in her dark pubescent moments when I was no longer a suitable confidante.

Always a serious cat, Max oddly tolerated Jess's vibrancy with good humor. As she ran past me, his head dangling down her back, he would look up from under half-closed eyelids and blink, his purr loud enough to be heard from where I stood. Between hunting expeditions in the basement, he would curl himself on her pillow and wait for her to come home to him. When he was hurt, he would come to me and stick his war wound in my face for examination, but the rest of the time, he was Jess's.

We moved again, not far this time, and Max launched himself into a frenzy of activity. There were doorways and windows to be examined and marked, and thirty acres to be checked for evildoers. Max was doing what he needed in his soul to do. Eventually the place became his, and peace reigned.

Jess's departure for college was traumatic for all of us, but more so for Max. He sulked on her bed, marked her furniture and the clothing she'd left behind, and punished her roundly when she came home for her first weekend visit. Eventually, however, she left again, and I closed the door to Jess's room. Though he would not be soothed, Max, grudgingly, moved onto my pillow.

Animals, with their short life spans, seem to age very suddenly. Max, at sixteen, was still robust and very much in control of his home. Almost overnight, however, he began to show his age. I swore that each time I looked at him he was a tad thinner and a bit quieter. The vet and I spoke in hushed tones about kidney failure and tumors. His all-day forays into the fields shortened to a walk from the front door to a chair on the back deck, where he would wait patiently to be noticed and allowed back inside. He spent hours sleeping behind the television. Finally, his body giving out, he stopped coming to my pillow at night. The vet came and gave him fluids and shook her head.

His last weekend, Jess came home from college to say goodbye to her lifelong friend. She holed up with him in the guest room and for two days tried to interest him in eating and drinking once again. Through her tears she begged me to do something, touching evidence of her still-unbounded (though misplaced) faith in "Mommy Magic." I syringed fluids into his mouth and left them alone together. From the kitchen, I called the vet. In the bedroom, Max had managed to get himself onto the bed and was sprawled across Jess's stomach, so dehydrated he was nearly flat. We sat in familiar silence and stroked his head while we waited for the vet to come.

The vet kissed the top of his head when I carried Max out to her truck. She then gave him the injection that released him. Jess's sobs echoed through the house.

The next day, bleary-eyed from a night of tears, my grown-up baby girl hugged me and returned to college. For one brief moment, we looked at each other and smiled. Memories too freshly aroused for discussion between us created a connection, fleeting, but full of promise.

Max's ashes are on my desk. I need him there to continue to soak up the occasional sadness as my newly adult daughter and I find solid footing for our relationship. I see him in my dreams, looking up at me from his spot on her shoulder, assuring me that life, in the end, is always good. We just need to love each other endlessly . . . and purr often and loudly.

JOANNE M. FRIEDMAN

WHO'S IN CHARGE HERE, ANYWAY?

*I*t was mid-March in northern Ohio, and we were about to get our first taste of spring. I could feel a tinge of spring fever in my bones and decided it would be a good time to introduce my ten-month-old female German shepherd, Bucky, to wilderness backpacking. I threw some gear into the back of the truck, packed in enough food for a three-day trek, and we were off to the Allegheny National Forest.

By noon, Buck and I were standing at the trailhead of the Hickory Creek Wilderness, an area that boasts a seventeen-mile loop trail through some very pretty forest. Bucky, in her usual fashion, was tugging furiously against her lead, wanting desperately to lunge down the trail. Having had no formal obedience training, Bucky's idea of a stroll in the woods consisted of covering three times as many miles as I did, tearing up and down steep ravines, charging through dense brush, and chasing after any critter that might come along.

Today, however, was going to be different, because Bucky was going to don a bright red backpack, one designed especially for large dogs. She would carry her own supplies, which consisted of five pounds of dry dog food. "Okay, Buck," I said, holding the end of her leash firmly under my foot. "This is your new backpack, sweetie." I laid it gently across her back, and fastened the straps around her chest. Bucky stood absolutely still, her soft brown eyes registering utter confusion. I patted her head, telling her it would be okay, and began to strap on my own pack. Bucky watched curiously. Taking the end of the leash in my hand, I said, "Come on, Bucky," and started down the narrow path. Suddenly Bucky understood. She had a job to do, and she trotted in front of me. Today she was a serious, dedicated working dog who was carrying a load and guiding Mom through unknown territory. I undid her leash, knowing that she wouldn't stray. She was very proud of herself, but no more so than I.

We hiked seven miles that day, both of us enjoying the lovely weather and a forest that was just beginning to show the promise of springtime. Late in the afternoon, we came upon a splendid campsite where people, probably Boy Scouts, had used fallen trees to build a seating area around a stone fire pit. Buck and I gathered firewood, and soon we were enjoying the warmth of a roaring fire.

As soon as Bucky smelled the hot dogs I had in my backpack, she started begging. The hike had made us both ravenous. I took some of Bucky's dog food out of her pack and gave it to her in a makeshift foil dish. If a dog is capable of looking indignant, Bucky certainly did. She walked over to the hot dogs and started whining. Fortunately, I'd brought extra, anticipating this very situation. "You can have a hot dog, Buck," I said, "but I think you'll be needing more than that, after today's workout." The hot dog served as a mere appetizer, followed by another hot dog, three hard-boiled eggs, half a bag of pita bread, a generous portion of cheddar cheese, and one granola bar. The dog food remained untouched. Though I'd planned on a three-day hike, we now had only enough food for one more day. I didn't care. We were having a great time, and Bucky had certainly earned her right to a "gourmet" meal.

We spent the evening enjoying the fire, and by 9:00 P.M. we were both ready for a good night's sleep. Within a few minutes, I'd set up our tiny tent, unrolled my forty-eight-by-twenty-inch sleeping mat, and arranged my sleeping bag on top of it. Then I took my extra set of clothing and made a soft bed for Bucky at the base of the tent. "Okay, Bucky." I called. "You can come in now."

And into the tiny tent lunged my seventy-eight-pound dog. She examined the arrangements and proceeded to spread out on my sleeping bag. "No, Buck, that's not how this works," I said, pointing to her bed at the back of the tent. Bucky has a way of ignoring me when she doesn't like what I'm saying. She'll bury her head against her side and simply go to sleep. And she did just that. I pushed, pulled, and cajoled, but Bucky was immovable. "Pleeeease, Bucky," I pleaded. "You have got to move!" I grabbed her collar and pulled, finally managing to drag her to one side of the tiny mattress. I now had all of ten inches to myself. While holding her in place, I grabbed the sleeping bag, threw it down on my portion of the mattress, and crawled in. I cuddled up to Bucky's back while trying to fit my rather ample rear end on the tiny space. I was too tired to care. "I love you, Buck," I whispered, and fell into a deep sleep.

By midnight, Bucky had managed to take over the entire mattress and most of the sleeping bag, and our relationship was beginning to tread on very thin ice. "I think your backpacking days are numbered, Buck," I growled to a snoring Bucky.

I was up at dawn, building a fire and making myself a much-needed cup of coffee. "I'm glad she doesn't like coffee." I mumbled to myself, while a well-rested Bucky ran happily about, exploring the forest.

Realizing that another night like the last would be more than my fifty-two-year-old body could endure, I decided we would head back to the truck around noon and arrive home in time for a good dinner.

By noon, we were on our way back down the trail, I carrying a much lighter load, and Bucky carrying her five pounds of dog food. As she had the day before, Bucky trotted proudly in front of me, paying strict attention to the trail, while I followed behind, my rather frayed state of mind drifting from one thought to another.

We'd gone about four of the seven miles when Bucky suddenly

started pulling on the leg of my jeans, and growling. "Stop that, Bucky." I said, thinking she wanted to play. She would often grab my leg in the yard when she wanted me to throw her Frisbee, but she'd never been so adamant. I started walking again, only to have her begin pulling even harder. Now she was growling in earnest and pulling me backward. I was afraid she would make me fall, and I envisioned being out here in the middle of nowhere with a broken leg. My voice rising in anger, I reprimanded her severely. "Bucky, I've had enough of this!" I scolded. "We're not playing; now cut it out." Bucky barked loudly and grabbed my leg again. Finally, thoroughly exasperated, I smacked her. Bucky was shocked. She'd never been hit before. Head down and tail between her legs she slouched off behind me, looking utterly dejected. I felt terrible for what I had done to my best friend. "Bucky, I'm sorry. I didn't mean to do that," I said, reaching out to her. "Come on, Buck, let's go," I said as cheerfully as I could, but she refused to come to me. I started walking again, hoping she would forget about what had happened. A few minutes later, I looked back to see Bucky still lagging behind. "Buck, I'm really sorry," I called, hoping she'd come running, but she was so upset, she wouldn't even look in my direction. I promised myself I'd make it up to her on the way home. I'd stop at McDonald's and buy her a cheeseburger, one of her favorite treats. I picked up my pace, now anxious to get back to the truck and make amends with Bucky.

Several miles later, we came upon a clearing, and the remnants of an old barn. It occurred to me that we hadn't passed a barn the day before. I looked back at Bucky, who was now lying in the middle of the trail, looking thoroughly disgusted. "Oh, Buck," I said, "I've gotten us lost. Is that what you've been trying to tell me?" I walked back to her, removed my pack, and sat down beside her. My heart ached over what I had done to my wonderful, faithful friend. How could I have been such a fool? I placed my head on her shoulder, and cried. Bucky's tail gave a slight wag, and she licked my hand.

How could she forgive me so easily, after what I had done? We sat there for several minutes, looking like two lost souls. Me with tears running down my face, and Bucky licking my hand, trying to make me feel better. "From now on, Buck, you're in charge of our backpacking trips," I said, hugging her tightly. "I promise I'll never let this happen again." I stood up, replaced my pack, and turned back down the trail. Bucky immediately jumped in front of me, thrilled to be in charge once again.

An hour or so later, Bucky made a left turn up another trail. There, on the side of a tree, was the off-white stripe, indicating a turn in the trail. It was the very same spot where Bucky had grabbed my leg. Feeling the fool, I followed her up the hill, and back to the truck.

On the way home, we stopped at McDonald's, and Bucky ate two cheeseburgers—hers and mine. And that night, after a long, hard day, we both collapsed in my bed, Bucky comfortably spread out with her head on the pillows, and I perfectly happy in my tiny little spot.

NANCY TOMAZIC

CREEPY IN THE HOUSE

I've discovered a wee case of prejudice in myself. People who don't have pets make me suspicious.

I can't help feeling this way. Plus, there are no listings for support groups or associations or twelve-step programs to help me deal with this narrow-minded way of thinking that I'm carrying around.

I see meetings for Parents Without Partners but not People Without Pets. People want to work on not having a partner, but they don't see the problem if they are petless.

Dogs and cats know things. Sometimes they share with us humans. We are better for it.

When my latest HMO assigned me a doctor, I interviewed him. I inquired about his credentials and his attitudes about this, that, and the other. Then he noted that he had no pets, no, uh-uh, didn't want them. "Creepy in the house," he said.

I tried to forgive him because he was from Tanzania, where he said pets and livestock were synonymous. But I found another doctor—an animal-loving, warm people person, who often would pat me on the arm when she was explaining something.

At a new faculty orientation I attended, we all went around the room introducing ourselves. It's still a requirement when new groups get together for any reason, I guess, even if it's to be told where and when to get ID pictures done and what the deadline is for handing in a syllabus. Every person in the room included in their families their respective cats and dogs. The odd bird. An iguana. Until we got to the dean. The dean was petless, by choice.

Not in mourning for a late Lab. No, he hated pets. *Creepy in the house,* I thought. If he were my department chair, I would probably have had to resign.

One of my best friends and her husband are childless and petless. They toil long hours and travel when they aren't working. They have lovely things, pristine rugs, and cannot keep a plant alive. When this best friend and I were growing up, she got a spaniel she named Lucky. Within forty-eight hours a car crushed the dog. For these reasons, I forgive them for not having an animal. But honestly? I think *they* think pets are creepy in the house.

The literature is loaded with articles about Pet Therapy. Pooches are taken to nursing homes now; suddenly there is hope and love in that world. Petting a dog or cat lowers our blood pressure. Having a dog or cat around means there is always a beating heart to listen to. Adding a new life to one's household isn't always easy because we usually outlive those furry, feathery, funny creatures we come to love so much.

A French poet in the last century insisted on walking a leashed lobster in the Tuileries gardens. He said he liked having a lobster for a pet because "they don't bark, and they know the secrets of the deep."

OK, another prejudice. Dogs and cats and birds are wonderful. Perhaps a ferret if one likes weasels. But a lobster? Definitely creepy in the house.

BEVERLY C. LUCEY

V
KNOWING WHAT'S BEST

In order to take care of others,
you have to take care of yourself.

Marjorie Haas

If your dog doesn't like someone, you probably shouldn't either.

AUTHOR UNKNOWN

A PACKAGE DEAL

"*Either that dog goes or I do!*"

I stood in my small kitchen, struck mute by his anger. He smiled triumphantly as my new puppy peed on the tile floor.

I felt a moment's guilt. Perhaps I had acted selfishly in buying this small fluffy sprite without considering his feelings. Maybe he would have preferred a manlier dog, like a shepherd or an Akita. I offered him a tentative smile, hoping he would get past his resentment and grow to accept my new fur child. Wasn't it almost impossible to resist a puppy?

"I'll give you three days to choose," he said. "And until then, I don't want to see you."

I searched his face for signs that this was a cruel joke. I couldn't believe, wouldn't accept that this was really happening. He knew I had always longed for a puppy and that my wish had finally come true. Yet he was spoiling what had promised to be a delicious Saturday filled with walks in the park and quiet cuddles.

I watched him leave, defeat clear in my eyes. We could have had so much fun raising the puppy together. Hope surged as he paused at my door.

"Everyone knows that apricot poodles are ugly," he said. "I wouldn't be seen dead with that dog."

It should have been a tough decision. My boyfriend and I had been going together almost four years, and we were talking about getting married. I had already seen the emerald and diamond heirloom ring. But as I looked down at the tiny scrap of peach fur with the large button eyes, my heart told me what I already knew. Bastian was here to stay.

At twenty-six, I had gone from being almost engaged to newly single, and it could have been a frightening, lonely time. Instead I had never felt more settled. I was pleased and surprised by how satisfying it felt to spend a Saturday night alone with my puppy and a video. I saw my girlfriends often, and Bastian seemed to fill any need for companionship beyond family and friends.

We passed a cold winter together and then I began dating. He was an affable man in his early thirties who insisted he loved animals. We shared a few quiet dinners before I invited him into my home and introduced him to Bastian. I now suspect that it was hate at first sight for them both. I wondered how much of an animal lover he could be when each time he visited he would request that I put "the dog" in the bathroom. "I'm more of a cat person," he eventually admitted. I was glad when Bastian chewed his Ray-Ban sunglasses. I wonder if he ever knew that, for me, the relationship was over the moment he "pretended" to feed Bastian a chili pepper. A few weeks later we parted friends.

There is a certain domestic fulfillment that comes from being young and sharing an apartment with a special dog. It didn't take long for us to again become content with our weekend routine of long walks in the park and shared Chinese takeout. Friends were concerned that I was becoming a "loner," but I had never been happier. I told them I would probably become "the dog woman of Cherry Hill," a cliché of the creepy old woman who lives with dozens of cats. In my version, I would live with dogs of all sizes and colors—a plethora of poodles.

"Children will gather in front of my house on Halloween and dare each other to ring my bell," I told them. "They will say my house is haunted and I'm a witch. I'll be a living legend."

No one laughed with me.

One Saturday night in early spring I received an unexpected call from a friend. He demanded that I get off the couch, get dressed, and be ready when he came to pick me up. I demurred, before switching to lame excuses and finally agreeing. I dressed quickly and let myself be spirited away for a night on the town.

His name was James. He met my friend and me at a bar and the attraction he and I felt was immediate. We passed the night casting subtle glances and pretending to ignore each other. He asked for my phone number, and I took his card instead. I had absolutely no intent of ever using it. He's too cute, too sure of himself, I reasoned. My life was great and I had never been happier. Why take a chance of screwing it up?

He said he could sense my reluctance when, worn down from pressure by our mutual friend, I finally called him. He sounded hesitant, too. We made plans for the following weekend and there was barely a moment in between where I didn't think about canceling our date. Saturday came and my stomach was queasy. When my doorbell rang I thought I would throw up. I ran to the mirror and realized that I was still wearing sweatpants and my face was bare. What had I been doing for the last hour? Had I really spent it daydreaming about how much I didn't want to go on this date?

The bell chimed again and Bastian barked furiously. I had no choice but to answer the door and invite him in.

At this point it must be said that anyone entering my home must greet Bastian first, as he would bark, dance, and jump until gratified. My tall date bent low to stroke my diminutive dog, informing me that he'd never had a pet.

Strike one, I thought.

I invited him to sit while I retreated to my bedroom, changing quickly and applying minimal makeup. It couldn't have taken more than ten minutes. I hurried back to the living room, eager to begin and, therefore, end our night. I will never forget the sight that awaited me. This long, handsome man whom I barely knew was stretched out on my couch, reading a magazine. Bastian was asleep in his lap.

"You look nice," he said when he saw me.

He gently moved Bastian onto the couch and covered him with a throw pillow. If either of us thought this action odd we gave no indication. Bastian seemed to smile in his sleep.

"Would you ever take my dog for a walk?" I couldn't help asking.

"Sure, why not?"

I didn't tell him that some guys found small dogs, especially poodles, offensive. I don't think he would have understood.

We had dinner at a new Italian restaurant. We talked about issues usually avoided on first dates and discovered we both wanted children and had similar values. I candidly told him that Bastian and I were a package deal.

"That's a nice package," he said.

After he walked me to my door (with a kiss on the cheek) I called my favorite aunt and told her I had met the man that I would marry.

We quickly became a couple.

One night, as happens in most new relationships, we began discussing our exes. I told him how Bastian had been the deal-breaker in my last two romances. He confirmed that he would be proud to be seen walking Bastian and that maybe some guys shun poodles because they are insecure about their manhood. "They worry too much about what other people think," he said.

Then he asked me if I could keep the knowledge that he some-times gave Bastian shoulder rides to myself.

What's not to love? The three of us were engaged within the year.

CHRISTINE M. CALDWELL

Like friends, it's the old ornaments that mean the most.
AUTHOR UNKNOWN

THE GRAND LADY

I t was forty years ago that my husband and I eagerly walked into a furniture store that was advertising its big Labor Day sale. We needed a recliner chair and had saved many months to buy one. Married only a few years, we deliberated over each purchase carefully. This one, we decided, would be a good investment. My husband worked long hours standing on his feet, and the recliner was his dream come true. That was all he talked about for weeks, the upcoming sale. Perhaps, for him, buying the chair represented his new life as a husband, a father, and a family man.

The red secretary was resting against a wall. I noticed it as soon as we entered the store. I felt an immediate connection, as I stood there, unable to move away. So tall, and majestic with its desk, slender drawers, and little cubbyholes. I lingered for a long time, memorizing every line of its structure. There was no way to explain that moment between the red secretary and myself. I couldn't even describe it to my husband.

"It certainly is something," he said, noticing my expression. "I've never seen anything like it. She's quite a grand lady."

We both looked at the price tag. It was beyond our means. Reluctantly I left the Grand Lady to look among the recliner chairs, but my heart was not into the search. My husband sat in one and then another but couldn't seem to make up his mind.

"Nothing really here," he said. "We'll try again another time."

"But there are so many to choose from," I told him.

He just shook his head. "Nothing I want to buy."

We passed the Grand Lady on the way out. I couldn't help my-self. I had to touch her one more time. My fingers gently passed over her regal structure. I was not a person usually taken by mate-rial things. But this was different. I felt this Grand Lady had some-thing to say to me. I could see myself sitting at her desk, perhaps writing my first story. I could see my daughter opening the two closed doors to discover the mysteries waiting within. I suspected the Grand Lady had lessons to teach me, something to share. She belonged in my life. But the practical side of me surfaced.

"Some things are beautiful to look at," I told myself. "You don't have to own them."

It was a week or two later when the delivery truck pulled up at my house to deliver the red secretary. Unknown to me, my hus-band had purchased it on an installment plan.

"The Grand Lady and you belong together," he said later.

In that moment, though married only a few years, I knew I would never have to explain myself to him. He understood the message in my eyes. We did without the recliner chair or a couch for a few years. But we were never sorry. The Grand Lady flat-tered each room in which she stood. Each area became special be-cause of her. And each dream seemed to become possible. When life threw me a curve, I'd sit at the desk and work it out, the Grand Lady watching over me. When impossible dreams seemed even more out of reach, I dusted her off carefully and remembered the day she was delivered to my home. Sometimes my husband would park his winter hat on her desk, or fill the cubbyholes with odds and ends. The children would often leave their books, school bags, or toys resting on her as if she were a shopping cart. She was patient with us through it all.

When my son moved to his own apartment, he had little furni-ture.

ther. Sadly enough, I had just started dating yet another "would-be dad" when I again moved Shane, this time to a rented mobile home. My son and I stayed in that trailer less than twenty-four hours, long enough for the gas heat to give out and for me to give up on having my own place.

With relief at first, I moved back to my parents' home. Graciously, they took in their grandson and me. At their place, the heat stayed on and the pipes didn't freeze. My son got his own room with his own grown-up bed. My parents were nearly always around to help me with him. My four brothers helped, too. Whenever they visited us, they played with their young nephew and showed him fatherly affection, just like my dad did.

But even with all that love surrounding my son, I wasn't very happy. Although many of my wild emotions stabilized through my Christian faith, I still had not learned that everything in life couldn't be and shouldn't be about me. In fact, while I sat outside with my mom one day, I complained bitterly.

My patient mother just listened while I ungratefully lamented my living arrangements. But then, as she gazed toward the quiet neighborhood street, Mother gently asked me, "Did you ever think that your living here is not for you?

"Maybe," Mother softly said, "God wanted Shane and you to live where you do for Shane's sake, not for yours." *For Shane's sake, not for yours.* I can still remember my mother's wise words. With her more mature eyes of faith, she saw that even when I didn't plan, someone else did. Mother understood that our heavenly Father meant my parents' place to be a stable base of blessing for Shane, not a burden for me. As if to affirm her faith that afternoon—and to help me see others through my blinding selfishness—God sent a sign, literally, to Mother and me.

While I talked with Mother outside, Shane was busy inside his grandfather's basement. Granddaddy's basement, full of car parts and other odds and ends, provided adventure for my son. And I don't recall how much time Shane worked in the basement that day while I vented my frustrations. But when he eventually emerged from his Papaw's world of tools and trinkets, Shane brought out a thin, splintery piece of wood. Proudly and silently, my little boy leaned his hand-fashioned creation against the curb in front of his grandparents' home. On the board, in bold red crayon, my son had written SPECIAL HOUSE.

BROOKE EVANS BALL

BEAT THE MARCHING
OF TIME

*A*nother visit back home with my parents, another milestone as I notice their shuffle has slowed while the concentration with which they eat their meals has grown. With each visit, their delight to see me is progressively underlined by their awe at the adult I have become.

There is something new to this visit, though, for I have brought my laptop computer. Every robotic chant of "You've got mail" brings them rushing in. They stand mute, their faces disapproving, as though the computer defied God in some mysterious way.

I am chatting with a friend at a café when my cell phone rings. It's my mother, telling me that the power in the building has shut off.

"Call the electric company," I say.

"It's your computer."

"My computer—what?"

"You know," she says. Her voice is the same one I used to hear not through my ears but through my skin. Now it is breathless, flustered. "The computer has burned up the switches—"

"Mom, my computer will go up in smoke long before it burns the switches for the entire building."

"So how come we have no electricity?"

The next day, as I am nursing a late-morning cup of coffee in the kitchen, my mother pulls out the chair across from me. The resolute squeeze of her lips tells me something serious is about to be discussed, maybe her living will.

"We got a wakeup call this morning," she says. "At five o'clock."

I look at her, waiting.

"It's your modem," she says to the dimwit I have become.

I sip my coffee, my eyes still upon her, registering the faint remains of the cheekbones of her youth, the cheekbones I inher-
ited, and which one day, too, will be no more.

"I don't understand," I say.

"We didn't order a wakeup call." Her tone means it is all self-
explanatory.

"What does this have to do with my modem?" I ask.

"Isn't it connected to the phone line? It has made the phone
ring!"

Slowly, I put down my cup. One, two, three. "My modem
doesn't make your phone ring. It only dials out for data."

"So why would suddenly our phone ring at five o'clock in the
morning?"

"I'll disconnect the modem whenever it's not in use. Okay?"

But the solution rattles my father. He picks up the end of his
phone cord, its plug loose on the desk like an old woman who has
lost her way home. Fumbling for the context in which to frame
his question, he examines its clear plastic tip, turning it around for
a better view.

"This is not meant to be plugged in and out," he finally says. "It
will break."

"All over America plugs are being plugged and unplugged," I
say. "Every day, all day. These plastic thingies are sturdy little creatures."

"It will break." Gently, he lays it down and turns to leave. But
the room—with his books, with his lemon-scented aftershave—is
still filled with his presence.

I follow him out and touch his shoulder. "Tell you what, I'll
stop in the hardware store, and use my own cord."

The next evening, while I'm out visiting a friend, my cell phone
rings. On the crystal display I identify my parents' number.

Indeed, it is my mother, and she is agitated. "We've told you,"
she says. "Now our phone is dead."

"At least you won't get any wakeup call at five o'clock in the morning," I say.

"You really have to do something about your computer. Since you arrived it has given us nothing but troubles."

"Okay, Mom." I sigh. "I'm sorry. I'll put it away."

For the next three years, when visiting, I stay with friends whose electricity, phone service—and well-being—remain unaffected by my laptop.

This year, when I arrive at my parents' apartment, they lead me to the study. There, on a polished oak stand, is a new computer, its large monitor gleaming through a clear vinyl protective cover, a pair of speakers flanking it.

"What happened?" I asked.

My mother replies in a no-nonsense, resolute tone I haven't heard in years. "Oh, on the way back from another funeral we stopped at the computer store. They gave us a good deal—"

"I'll e-mail to the grandchildren," my father cuts her. The creases on his cheeks bunch up with pride. "And it will cost nothing. Your sister's son will show me how."

My nephew is nine. I want to ask how the power and phone lines will withstand the extra traffic, but something swells up in me. In my head I hear the drumbeat of time receding. Unexpectedly, unknowingly, my parents have made it turn around, go someplace else. I don't remember ever being so proud of them.

"I want to improve my bridge game." There is a new spark in my mother's eyes as she points to a stack of software packages. She fumbles behind the computer and plugs it into the electric socket. "Just install these and show me how they work."

But as I lift the monitor cover and then turn on the switch, I can't read the screen. My eyes are misted.

TALIA CARNER

LIFE WITH HOPE

*E*veryone has an unforgettable character; one of my favorites is Hope. We first met when I was a fresh-out-of-high-school cashier and she was an about-to-retire cashier. We were both assigned to the first drive-thru bank. The Metropolitan Bank installed one on the corner of Main and Market streets in Lima, Ohio.

Hope was special. She was a slight woman, maybe five-foot-nothing and ninety pounds soaking wet, but she was energetic, feisty, caring, and somewhat flighty. She and I established a combination of coworker-mother-daughter-good-friend relationship and it worked well. We didn't always know who was the mother and who was the daughter, and life with Hope was anything but dull.

Moving into our new space was certainly not dull, either. The teller drive-thru, newly constructed and smelling of fresh paint, had a few bugs in it, but we were to move in and work things out as they happened.

Hope and I had just stocked the tiny vault with our first cash, turned around to our windows, and faced a line of grim Lima policemen armed with shotguns. Another policeman came charging into the walk-up and scared Hope, who threw the handful of bills into the air and put her hands over her head. Obviously one of the bugs was in our alarm system.

We saw the Lima police quite often, and Hope and I adjusted to guns pointed at our heads.

We both dove under our desks the day the man tried to drive his fourteen-foot RV under our thirteen-foot canopy and shook the entire building. The shocked look on his face as his truck stopped its forward progress and the hood ornament rose upward toward the roof is ingrained in my memory. Hope's wide-eyed exclamation, "men drivers," sent us under our desks again with laughter.

Laughter was a big part of working with Hope. For some reason things just seemed to happen to her and she told everything. After working with her for two weeks, I think I knew her better than my own sibling. For example, she told of her childhood and having rheumatic fever.

This story I remembered vividly the day she became so angry with a belligerent customer that Hope fainted dead away on the carpet at my feet. I just knew her heart, damaged by rheumatic fever, had chosen that moment to stop working, and I was locked in a room with a dead Hope and a line of impatient customers. She survived and added one more story to her collection. The customer never returned to our windows.

Hope could tell a story like no one else. One of her favorites involved a tornado that hit part of Lima in the 1940s or early fifties. She and her husband, Walt, almost newlyweds, decided to drive around and see what damage the storm had done. Walt tensely looked for downed power lines and anything that could hurt them or his new Buick. Hope simply enjoyed the sights. She spied a peaceful mallard sitting in the midst of the poststorm urban chaos and, not wanting Walt to miss the sight, shouted, "Duck!"

Walt ducked and drove his new Buick over the curb and across the sidewalk and parked it under someone's picnic table.

Walt still tightens his jaw as Hope tells her duck story. I think he is visualizing the grillwork on his Buick.

Hope came into my life when I needed her most. I was a vulnerable half-woman half-child taking my first steps into the world. She gave me her friendship and encouragement and two years of nonstop days filled with humor and the unexpected.

We eventually went our separate ways until I read in the newspaper of her son's death. At the funeral home people filled the building and a line led out the front door. Hope didn't have any smiles or stories that day.

This was the day her friends returned a bit of what she had given to them. We gave her hugs, words of caring, and strength to go on, just as she had done for all of us.

DAWN GOLDSMITH

You don't get points for intent, only for results.
ANNIE MORITA

REAL WORK

I have had many paying jobs over the years, and I enjoyed most of them, but sooner or later I left those jobs. For some time now I have been doing my "real" work, raising six children. There have been occasional lapses when I work for money and that little emotional boost that comes from being valued by the world's standards.

Sometimes when people ask me, "What do you do?" I just say, "Everything." No one has been able to respond to that yet.

When I work at jobs other than mom, I get more respect. My family pitches in more, and my husband really does give me more deferential treatment, though he hotly denies it. I definitely get more rest. When I have turned my attention to raising my children full-time, my standing has gone down a notch or two in some people's eyes. That's OK, we don't have those folks to dinner. They probably wouldn't appreciate mac and cheese with weenies anyway.

I confess, some days I throw around job titles. I compound the very problem I complain about, contributing by tacking on meaningless "stuff" to what I know to be the most important job I will ever do. I like the warm glow that it gives me. Saying you are tired because you were up "working" all night seems to be more of an accomplishment than admitting those dark circles are because you were rocking a cranky baby until all hours.

You can't resign from your real work. Just last week I was so tired and frustrated with this thankless task of child-rearing that I went outside and hid in my minivan. After brushing the cracker crumbs off the backseat, I wedged myself in between the two carseats and pulled the shades down. I thought those wild thoughts all moms have when they know the gas tank is full and no one can really stop them from driving away.

But then the two-year-old opened the front door. I tried very hard not to hear her, but my mommy radar was still fully functional even though my nerves were frayed and my voice inoperable. Years of on-the-job training told me she wasn't wearing shoes and no one was watching over her.

I sighed and decided it was quite impossible to run away when you are a mom. No one else would take this job.

I wouldn't let them.

DONNA STONE

THE CHRISTENING GOWN

I had been married only a few months when my grandmother showed me the handmade cotton baby christening gown. It was off-white and had not yellowed or torn. It was bordered with delicate eyelet designs, and I could imagine it decorating a porcelain doll. Or a precious child.

"Someday," she said, "I'll give it to you for my great-grandbaby."

I touched the gown and nodded. My husband and I loved sifting through dark antique shops and finding treasures at flea markets. And here was a family heirloom, full of memories and possibilities of new ones. I looked at the gown often when I visited my grandmother, imagining how it would look on my own child at our baby's dedication.

Three years later, after a disappointing time of anticipating a pregnancy that seemed like it would never happen, my husband and I left the doctor's office to tell my grandmother that, at last, she would indeed be a great-grandmother in a few months. She presented me with the gown, like a queen presenting a knight with his first suit of armor.

"Your great-grandmother made this while she was expecting me," my grandmother explained. "I wore it when I was a baby, my first time to be presented to God and society."

As the firstborn grandchild and her only granddaughter, I felt a great deal of responsibility for the baby growing inside and the heirloom my grandmother so proudly passed on. As my husband and I worked to decorate the nursery, I laid the gown inside a pale yellow bassinet I'd purchased at a garage sale. It was easy to imagine the beautiful baby who would soon be sleeping quietly.

Two months later, I learned that my pregnancy had been an illusion, merely a desperate measure that my mind wanted so badly, telling my body to respond appropriately. After we changed doctors, my new doctor became concerned at not hearing a heartbeat. A blood test was run and the shocking news given me as I sat alone in the room. I had not been pregnant.

I cradled the gown in my arms, standing in the nursery we had already begun. I felt as if I had failed as a wife and granddaughter. Would I ever hold a child, ever see it wear the gown? Quickly, I gave away everything we'd bought. Friends who had babies on the way were better able to use the things than we were. I couldn't face the room again for a long time.

But the gown was placed in a small antique strongbox. My baby hope chest. Beside it lay the solid-gold earrings my mother gave me, passed on from her great-grandmother to the first daughter in each generation that married. I wore them on my wedding day, as my great-great-grandmother had done, a gift from her fiancé, who had poured and molded them himself. I had hoped to pass them on to my own daughter someday. Every so often, I would take out the gown and hold it in my lap. Eight years passed and I found myself finally unable to touch it.

My brothers had children. My cousins had children. I was grateful that my grandmother had not asked me to give away the gown, this special heirloom waiting for a small body to caress.

Then, in 1991, my husband and I began adoption classes. I often sat on the floor of the future nursery, took the gown out, and wondered how my great-grandmother had felt in anticipation of her first child.

Michelle, my daughter, arrived in a flurry of joy and excitement. But at nine months old, she had outgrown the gown before she had the chance to wear it. I bought a new dress for her to wear at her baby dedication one December morning. Again, I put my grandmother's gown away.

One day, my three-year-old daughter came to me, proudly holding her snow-white bear that we had given her the day we first met her. The bear wore the christening gown. My daughter wore a smile.

"Look what I found. Isn't it pretty?"

I pulled both daughter and bear into my lap. "Yes, it's very pretty." I told her the story of the gown and our years of praying for a daughter like her.

"Someday, I hope your child, my grandchild, will wear this special gown."

Michelle smiled at me. She carefully undressed the bear and put the gown back in the box.

Every so often, we take it out of the box and imagine the baby who will someday wear it. Yet, I've always wondered how my precious daughter would have looked in the gown.

This Christmas, my mother made porcelain dolls for each of her five granddaughters. The dolls were to resemble the girls. Skin tone, hair color, eyes. I saw my daughter take form in my mother's loving work. When the dolls were done, she allowed her granddaughters to choose their doll's outfit.

"I'm afraid Michelle chose a pretty complicated one," my mother said. "I don't know if I can make it."

She showed me the pattern. "It's a christening gown," she explained. "Lots of eyelet lace. I just don't think I can do it."

My heart pounded. "I think I have an idea."

I slipped the gown from its resting place. Someday, I felt sure a grandbaby or few would wear it. But for now, at last, I could see how my daughter might have looked.

The gown fit perfectly, flowing down the doll in antique eyelet. I cried as I took pictures of the doll and gown, of my mother standing beside my daughter as she held the doll.

I felt sure that my grandmother, who passed away five years ago when Michelle was three, would approve. And I had finally seen the gown on my own daughter, and it was beautiful.

KATHRYN LAY

YOU WON'T HEAR ME CRYING

I've been a parent for what seems like an interminable length of time.

Okay, so it's only been nineteen and a half years—a flash in the pan compared to what my parents have endured—but it's hard to remember a time when I wasn't a mom.

Although I love my children just as much as the next mother, sometimes I don't cry when other mothers are crying.

Is there something wrong with me? Do I have faulty maternal wiring? Am I hardhearted? Am I lacking?

It occurred to me that I wasn't conforming to the Mother Code when my friend (and neighbor) began succumbing to regular bouts of hysteria over the prospect—six months in advance, mind you—of her daughter graduating from high school, leaving home, and going to college.

You see, I couldn't wait until my oldest child did just that. (At least, I hoped he would do just that. I didn't want him sticking around like the middle-aged guy in the TV commercial who is planted on his parents' sofa demanding fresh potato chips. Now *that's* something to cry about!)

My friend was so distraught over her daughter's not-so-imminent departure that, one night while driving home from work, she succumbed, yet again, to hysterics, which impaired her driving. Her van was weaving all over the road. A state trooper just happened to be behind her. The trooper pulled over my grief-stricken friend and demanded that she submit to a field sobriety test.

So there she was, my friend, the teetotaler, walking the line; touching fingertip to nose; trying, in earnest, to explain to the officer that she wasn't drunk, just experiencing a premature onslaught of maternal separation anxiety.

I never shed a tear when my oldest son graduated from high school. In fact, I was pretty much euphoric over the prospect. I was excited—for him and for my husband and me. I felt an utter sense of relief when I saw him standing in the commencement line, looking spiffy and official in his cap and gown. He'd shown up; he'd made it; there was a coveted diploma with his name on it. I think it was the first time that I'd breathed easily in two years.

When people asked me: "Are you sad that he's graduating?" "Do you miss him now that he's away at college?" "Isn't it lonely without him?" I was tempted to answer honestly and say "No" to all of the above. But I figured answering in such a manner would label me a maternal pariah, albeit an honest one, so I lied and said, "Yes."

It has occurred to me that my willingness to let go of my children isn't anything new. When my oldest child was just three and a half years old I finagled his way into nursery school, which only accepted four-year-olds.

Fourteen years ago, when my friends were freaking out because their babies were heading off for kindergarten, I, conversely, was of the "What is this half-day stuff? Can't they go all day long?" frame of mind.

I guess I've always been ready and willing to move on to the next stage, and I don't think that's bad, just the natural order of things.

My husband and I have discussed our willingness (no armtwisting required here) to let go. Is it a character fault? Are we somehow lesser parents than the moms and dads who are felled by empty-nest syndrome? I don't think so.

Being a mother has been, and still is, the most time-consuming, exasperating, yet rewarding and wonderful thing that I've ever undertaken in my life. I have given it 100 percent and then some and consider it a good, healthy sign that, when the time comes, my children and I are in complete agreement: It's time to pack your bags and move on! If my children go on to become well-adjusted and self-sufficient adults, then I'll consider my mission accomplished and well done.

And, yes, I do cry. Lots. In fact, my husband would attest that I'm capable of being a world-class sobber. But I don't cry because my children are moving on to the next stage of their life. No. I cry because my children have been hurt or mistreated. I cry because my children are using poor judgment or selling themselves short. I cry when my children do stupid, dangerous things. But I will *never* cry because they want to spread their wings and move on.

My husband and I will be empty-nesters before we know it.

So, what's that going to be like when the kids have all flown the coop and it's just the two of us? No more distractions, no sibling brawls to referee, no late-night pacing and frantic fingernail-biting, wondering where a kid is and whether he's managed to wrap himself around a tree.

Whatever will I do with those hours that were formerly devoted to laundry and dirty dishes, familial mediation and crisis intervention?

Hmmm . . . I'll just have to wait and see, but methinks I'll like it just fine!

CINDI PEARCE

VI
A LOVING TOUCH

Love is the only thing that keeps me sane.

Sue Townsend

LOVE NOTES

*O*ne of the ways my husband and I try to keep our romance alive is to leave each other little love notes. Sometimes they are in plain sight, and other times we try to put them where the other will be happily surprised. The notes aren't often wordy. Just short little reminders of why we have chosen each other.

I have often hidden love notes in his suitcase for a business trip, discreetly tucked in undergarments to delay the discovery. I have also found such notes in my own suitcases on occasion. Once, a note was secretly tucked in my bowling ball to find on an evening out with friends.

The weather often determines what time I will go in to work. I have the luxury of a flexible job, where I am able to arrive late and make up missed time later. Recently, I awoke to find about six inches of snow had fallen. I immediately decided to wait until the snowplows had a chance to clear the roads, and to hear the weather report before venturing out. I did, however, go out and clear the accumulation of snow off my car. When I came back into the house, my husband was just putting on his coat to leave for work. A hug and a kiss and he was gone. Having already made coffee, I poured it into my travel mug. It's always just the right amount. I use the mug to measure out the water, so none goes to waste. I added sugar and some cream and stirred the mixture. I put the lid on as well because sometimes I'm a little clumsy and I didn't wish to push my luck.

Having a little free time to spare, I checked my e-mail and

browsed the Internet a little while. The snow continued to fall, so I was unconcerned with the time. The weather report revealed a possibility of six to eight additional inches' accumulation. Hearing that I decided to take a day's vacation and remain in the sanctity of my home. All the while, I drank my coffee. One gulp seemed to be a little bit thicker than the rest, but I figured I hadn't stirred it quite enough.

As soon as I logged off the Internet the telephone rang. It was my love. He was glad to hear I was safe and sound. We were having a nice chat when he asked me, "Did you get my note?" I had not seen any note, so I responded, "Where did you leave it?" I peered around the kitchen countertop, seeing no note. "I left it in your coffee cup." With this I started laughing hysterically. I took the top off my coffee cup and fished out what was left of the note.

Barely legible I could read the words "Good mor— babe. Hope y— slept ———. ——— wait to see ——— —n. Love you. —ove, ———."

MARCIE HENDERSON

A house needs a grandma in it.
LOUISA MAY ALCOTT

GROOVIN'.

"**W**hat do you mean, he has other plans?" I asked my daughter. "He was supposed to visit with me today."

We were talking about my nine-year-old grandson, Ryan. He always jumped at the chance to visit me. We played with the dog, Sparky, in the backyard. We talked to the birds, chased the squirrels, and worked at my writing desk. Sometimes we just sat next to each other, perfectly comfortable in our silence. On special occasions we would go out for dinner. Just the two of us. Ryan always ordered double hamburgers with extra pickles. He usually used a half bottle of ketchup on his french fries.

"He has a playdate," my daughter replied.

I stiffened at the word "playdate." For some reason, it annoyed me. Play was play. Spontaneous. Unplanned. Often uncontrollable. What was this "date" thing? But I had another reason for my annoyance. There had been many playdates recently. One visit to a classmate after school. Another running with a friend, under hose water on a hot day. In between baseball, basketball, jumping in leaves, and exploring assorted mysteries only nine-year-olds could discover, there were dozens of offers for playdates. And very little time for me.

"Where's Ryan?" became the familiar query.

"Playdate," became the expected response.

Who was that flash racing down the driveway, with a basketball in one hand and a baseball in the other? "Hi, Grandma," Ryan would say, planting a quick kiss on my cheek as he sped away from the house. "What about our trucking business?" I called to him, though he was out of earshot. When he was younger, Ryan and I spent hours operating our trucking business. We'd line up our plastic trucks, put them in garages, and spend hours traveling from the kitchen to the living room delivering our goods. Often, after business hours, we drew chalk pictures on the front sidewalk. Ryan didn't seem to enjoy that as much anymore. Nor the quiet times. He grew restless. "What else is there to do?" he'd ask. But then when we found something else to do, like a game of Scrabble, and just when the game was getting good, the telephone would ring. It would be for him. When he returned to the game, he would look at the Scrabble board as if it were a bowl of hot cereal. He hated hot cereal. He didn't have to tell me where he was headed. "Playdate."

Wasn't I his buddy also? Had he forgotten the sleepover when he called me a Viking warrior because I slept with the eggbeater on my pillow? Ryan did not want the dog jumping on the bed while he was asleep. The dog was afraid of the whirrrring sound of the eggbeater. Ryan considered it a weapon of war with which I had outwitted the enemy. But those exciting moments between us did not come as often anymore.

One night when he was visiting, a song played on the radio. He sang the words and began to move to its rhythm. I joined him. Dancing in my kitchen was my favorite pastime. We each took a part of the room as we spun around, laughing, clapping our hands, keeping a beat to the rock music.

"You like this music?" Ryan asked, surprised.

"I like all music," I responded.

"You're a good dancer," he said. "Maybe next time you come to my house, we'll do some groovin'."

I think we have a playdate.

HARRIET MAY SAVITZ

FIRED INTO HEAVEN

For seven years I'd been crewing yachts as a cook, cruising both coasts of the Americas, along the Mediterranean, through the Caribbean, and into the Pacific. By the time I reached the *Virginian*—a 204-foot Dutch-built yacht out of England—I was tired. She was my third boat in a year.

On the *Virginian* my position as second chef was hard, but I had a large, appreciative crew, an open kitchen budget, and a beautiful galley. Often after work I'd go to the gym with the deck crew, go out with the girls, and swap philosophy books with the engineers. I felt that I'd finally found the right job.

Three months into the job our new schedule indicated we were going to have a very busy summer with many highbrow clients. My head chef left for personal reasons, and the *Virginian*'s owners launched a full-scale search around London to find a replacement of his caliber. In a pub one night, over a pint, the captain said the owners thought my presence might be an obstacle for some of the candidates under consideration. But under the haze of thick English beer, I didn't pay him much mind. So a few weeks later when I was summoned to the captain's office, handed a month's salary and written notice, I was stunned. The captain explained the owners had found a chef who came with an assistant in tow.

"No big deal," he said, shrugging, "we just don't need you anymore."

My heart fell as if I'd stepped out of the crow's nest into thin air.

"Oh, by the way," he said, cutting a glance out the door, "your replacements will be here in an hour."

My body hummed the way the refrigerator did right before it went on the fritz. In fact, the fridge was full of half-done projects, just like the rest of my life. I'd just moved into a cabin with my best friend and had just started a "special" friendship with another crew member, and here I was being fired.

The English steward, the one crew member I'd never hit it off particularly well with, found me in the fridge sobbing fiercely over a pot of steaming boeuf bourguignon. Too distraught to hide my misery, even in front of his hard, incredulous face, I wept harder.

"Look," he said, "this has absolutely nothing to do with you."

I cried harder.

"Mishele," he shook me by the shoulders, "stop this! Go to your cabin, put on your street clothes, and make yourself up. Walk off this boat holding your head high." He pulled me from the fridge and pointed me toward the door.

The captain said I could stay on board and promised to help me find another job, but I just wanted off. My cabin mate Anna packed my bag and sneaked my stuff out, promising to break the news to everyone else later. I just couldn't handle the goodbyes. Besides, I'd see them all in the South of France, where the *Virginian* was headed, because it was also where unemployed crew found jobs.

In the back of a large black English cab, tears sheeted down my face. But before I could break into a sob, I felt a blanket-like warmth envelop me, giving way to a floating sensation. Almost like being lifted. So noticeable was the feeling that I stopped crying. As the cab drove away from the pier, words swirled around me . . . "Mishele, we've got to go."

"Where to?" asked the cabby.

His words brought me back from my dreamlike state. Having just been fired and made homeless in one fell swoop, I had no idea, but started to laugh. "Where to?" was a good question.

"Travel agent," I said.

By the next evening, I lounged on my friend's restaurant terrace in Provence slurping pink wine. The second day on the terrace a card dropped from my wallet. I hadn't remembered putting it there, but since the number was for a job placement agency for yacht crew, I rang them up. Within a matter of hours, I faxed an outdated résumé and spoke three times with the captain of a 174-foot sailboat who coincidentally needed a chef. Over my umpteenth glass of rosé, I accepted the job.

I met them in Monaco for a short stint before the boat sailed to Viareggio for a two-month renovation in an Italian shipyard. My job was less than perfect. However, during the boat's stay in dry dock, I met a tall, curly-haired Italian who spoke English. While he was driving me all over Tuscany in a rickety, powder-blue Fiat, we found love.

Had my departure from the *Virginian* not been forced, I wouldn't have made those calls from a terrace in Provence, or taken the job that put me in Alessandro's path, which means I wouldn't be engaged and living in Italy. What had seemed so unjust, so earth-shattering, turned into a beautiful life I could never have planned. It was in the firing that I discovered heaven on earth.

MISHELE ABELL

STOCKPILE

Born at eleven pounds, eleven ounces and a full twenty-four inches, my son was bigger at birth than my twin daughters were at three months. Remembering the weightless bundles they made at half his heft and six inches less his height, I found the bulk of my son's newborn body a solid surprise.

My girls stayed on the small side, making me feel as if I was able to somehow wring every precious atom out of their babyhood. But from the very beginning my son's exceptional size seemed to accelerate his infancy. I secretly mourned that he never fit into the napkin-sized newborn diapers that I had so neatly arranged in the drawer, anticipating his arrival. I donated them wistfully to a neighbor's baby, along with an unused stack of outfits that he was never small enough to wear. When he wore a size 2T and weighed as much as his two-year-old sisters at only six months, part of me felt cheated, taunted, by his too-quick transformation from infant to boy. I kept his tiniest booties as convincing, if unbelievable, evidence to myself that he really was small once.

Propelled on a trajectory of purposeful movement from his leg-kicking start, he reveled in the wider boundaries outside the confines of my body. In the hospital, totally unlike his sisters, he chafed at swaddling blankets and squirmed, rocked, and shook until a fist or foot broke free, and kept wriggling until he lay victorious in his bassinet, his wrappings cast aside like eggshells.

He was never a lap-baby. He never liked to be rocked. To be soothed, he had to be walked, and held out so he missed nothing. He disliked swings, jumpers, and bounce chairs. These moved but didn't go anywhere. Speeding cars and jogging strollers were much more to his taste. Once he took his first steps at nine months and gained access to surroundings that had so long eluded him, he became a very happy child.

I became a nervous wreck.

The world has become his mountaineering expedition. To him, furniture was made to climb, countertops designed to be scaled, and heights created to be leaped from. He rolls off beds, falls down stairs, and stands in the toilet bowl.

Now, at eighteen months, he rarely sits still long enough to finish a book. Cuddling is not typically on his agenda. He is what my friends call "busy," restless and exuberant, thrilled by the world and definitely happy to run free from the shelter of his mother's arms. If I am the sun, he is very much a planet with a far-flung orbit.

While I frequently find myself looking longingly at his back, as he tears off in pursuit of something far more interesting than his mother, I sincerely respect his independence and energy. I know, beyond a doubt, that these traits will serve him well, and I am glad for them.

But there is a small part of me that secretly wishes he were more sedate and less bold. Not just because it would give me fewer heart attacks if I saw him successfully scaling my lap more often than the bookshelf, but mostly because I know he may be my last child, my last baby. That knowledge sends some hungry part of me into a hoarding mode, greedily gathering every hug and kiss, every quiet moment of physical closeness into a sort of maternal stockpile. It is this part of me that wants what he doesn't. It yearns to constrain him, to hold him, cradle him, cuddle him, rock him, and consume the very babyness of him while it still clings to him.

Yet, today, quite unexpectedly, he sits quietly with me, his head on my chest, totally absorbed with pulling on the buttons of my shirt. My lunch cools, forgotten on the counter. I smooth fine blond hair and bury my nose in the soft spot where his neck meets shoulder. I kiss the freely submitted still-baby cheek. He laughs and smiles, eyes only for me, jibber-jabbering in his sweet, still-baby voice. I inhale every detail of him. When something across the room catches his eye he is down, off and running, without a second thought or backward glance, careening into his customary orbit. His absence leaves my lap lighter and suddenly cool, and my heart warmed by the weight of a stockpile grown suddenly large and very adequate.

KAREN C. DRISCOLL

If you've ever had a mother and if she's given you and meant to you
all the things you care for most, you never get over it.
ANNE DOUGLAS SEDGWICK

THE MUSIC OF
MY MOTHER'S LIFE

When our first child was born, my mother came to help for just a week and stayed for three. This grandchild, not her first, she dubbed "The Peach," and so she was called for many years. My mother rocked her Peach in the rosy light of dawn, hoping I could catch a few more winks; yet I woke often in those weeks to hear my mother crooning not a lullaby, but the songs of the twenties and the thirties, which she knew so well. The rocker creaked now to, now fro, while she sang:

"Oh, my man, I love him so . . ."

If "My Man" did not quiet the Peach, my mother would go on with a medley of songs that included "I'm Dancing with Tears in My Eyes" and "Pagan Love Song."

I would lie in bed remembering the times she sang her songs to me, made light of all my sorrows with "Jeepers, creepers . . . ," and chided me with "You're a Sweet Little Headache." I loved to hear her singing to her grandchild, and when the Peach had settled down once more, I heard my mother moving briskly around the kitchen where she prepared a breakfast only a giant could eat.

"You don't have to fix me such a big breakfast, Mom," I'd say, looking aghast at the mound of food she set before me each day.

"But that's why I came," she'd protest. "To take care of you. To see to it that you get your strength back. I'm here to see to it that you 'eat an apple every day . . .' "

She sang her way through all the daily chores in our house. Over the noise of the vacuum cleaner, I would hear her warble one or another "golden oldie," and when the Peach came down with colic, it was my mother who walked her around and around the house, singing:

"the music goes 'round and 'round . . ."

When the day came for her to leave, my mother packed her bags while I loaded her down with promises that if I ever needed her I would "just whistle."

I whistled for her two years later when our son was born. This time she sang her heart out to her "Little Buckaroo." I had forgotten that my mother knew so many cowboy songs, and soon I, too, was singing, "Ride, Tenderfoot, Ride" as I rocked our son to sleep.

Once, in a jealous snit, the Peach asked my mother if she would sing a lullaby "just for me, Grandma," and my mother obliged by belting out:

"C'mon along and listen to . . ."

The Peach pounded on her pillow, shrieking with delight, while my mother strutted around the bedroom, singing the only lullaby she knew. I finally had to go in there and settle our daughter down with "Go Tell Aunt Rhody," which my mother always said was an old lady's song.

For the first few days of her stay with us, my mother plied me once again with breakfast only a giant could eat and never failed to remind me as I sipped a glass of wine to "stay away from bootleg booze . . ."

After the first week, my mother did not rise at dawn as she had done before and oftentimes I found her dropping off to sleep in the chaise longue where she had settled down to watch the Peach at play in the yard. When she began to take "just a second to catch my breath" after needlessly vacuuming the rugs for a second time in one day, I suggested that she need not stay if all the work was just too much, but she insisted she belonged with me.

And when one day she stumbled coming up the basement steps carrying a load of freshly ironed, Perma-Prest sheets, I demanded that my mother rest and said that *I* would take care of *her* for a change.

She eased up a little on the chores, then forced herself to stay in bed until eight when she "had to" get up and give her Buckaroo his morning bath. After just two weeks of hardships, my mother decided that she would go home.

"I'm sorry that I can't stay longer," she said, "but I guess it's time 'the old gray goose is dead.' " Even though she giggled when she said it, I felt a chill wind inch its way toward my heart and gently reminded my mother that there was a lot of life in the old girl yet.

Four years later, we had another child. This time, my mother did not come to help, but sent a bunch of roses to our house. She had tucked a card in with the gift. It read: "Give my love to that million-dollar baby and come see me when you can. Love, Mom."

I now sing the songs that my mother knew so well. My children tell me that I'm "out of it" and laugh at lyrics warning them to "button up your overcoat. . . ." But just the other day, I heard the

Peach belt out a few lines from "Lullaby of Broadway" and I was glad to know that all the music of my mother's life still goes " 'round and 'round . . ."

And it comes out here.

JEAN JEFFREY GIETZEN

CAN WE TALK?

*T*he first time I went out with Jeff, I had no idea that I was on a date. I had no idea because, unlike the typical "dates" I had been going on, there was no tension, no stumbling into awkward silences, and no low-level straining to discern whether I was making a good impression.

We met, as we had planned to, outside one of my favorite restaurants and immediately fell into easy conversation for hours. I had the odd sensation that somehow Jeff was not a new person in my life, but an old friend who I simply hadn't met until that evening. We shared stories about places we had traveled, funny and strange dates we had been on, and our goals for our careers. One topic of conversation smoothly segued into the next. We might not have been able to dance all night, but we could have easily talked all night.

How had this wonderful guy fallen into my social orbit? He had called me at work one day out of the blue, having just moved to town and gotten my phone number from a mutual friend in another city. When Jeff told her that he was moving to Los Angeles, she made his job of meeting friends easy: She tore off a small scrap of paper, wrote five names and numbers on it, and gave it to him. She put a star next to the name at the top, saying, "Start with Judy, she knows all the rest and will get you in touch with them."

Jeff walked around with the note in his wallet for several weeks before picking up the phone to call that starred name on the list. He called, sounding casual. "I got your name from Becky," he said. "I thought we might get together so I could see what you look like." I could have been insulted, but his friendly tone made me think instead, *Okay, pal, I'm up to that challenge!*

During our first dinner together, I was so comfortable with Jeff that I did something I never would have done had I believed myself to actually be on a date: I ordered spinach quiche, and instructed him point-blank to tell me if any got on my teeth. And after dinner, I not only ate my own ice cream, I polished off his as well.

Given all that, it's probably odd that when I got home that night, I thought to myself, *What a great guy. Too bad I'll never see him again.* It never occurred to me that Jeff would call a second time. After all, he had accomplished his mission: He had seen what I looked like.

Jeff also happened to call during the only period of my single life when I was dating several men at once. Frankly, I was dizzy with my newfound, novel popularity, and frankly, Jeff was young, with no car, no job, still living at home. I was husband shopping, and as much as I liked him, he didn't seem like a prospect.

So I was thrilled when Jeff called again a week later. He appeared different to me next time. When we first met his attire of jeans and a polo shirt underscored his youthfulness. The second time he arrived fresh from a day of job hunting, wearing a suit. I then noticed how handsome he was, and that he had attractive, masculine shoulders.

Hey, maybe this could *be a date!* I suddenly realized, struck by the notion that a date could, under certain rare circumstances, really feel like a natural phenomenon. But I nearly blew it that night. Over dinner, I tried to buoy Jeff's spirits after his disappointing day of fruitless job searches. I assured him that he would be employed soon. At the end of the evening, I blundered, "Call me when you get a job!" Now to me, it was perfectly clear that I meant he should call me to share the happy news of his employment. But what he heard was, *"Don't* call me *until* you get a job!"

So I didn't hear from him for a week. Then two weeks. In the meantime, the men I had been dating began to pale in comparison to Jeff. The other guys may have all had their own cars, their own apartments, and jobs, but they didn't have a dry sense of humor. They didn't share my values. They couldn't keep the conversation flowing as smoothly as good friends always could.

I finally called Jeff. "I thought you didn't want me to call you until I had a job," he said, sounding surprised to hear from me.

"What? That's ridiculous!" I was startled and embarrassed to realize I had unintentionally hurt his feelings. "I only wanted to share your good news when it happened, that's all!"

Fortunately, since then my instincts about what may hurt the male ego have been honed to a finer degree. Although Jeff still occasionally kids me about my thoughtless remark, a small throwaway line potentially as fateful as that little piece of paper with my name and phone number on it.

While we dated, Jeff would sometimes ask, "Do you ever worry we'll run out of things to talk about?" But after fifteen years of marriage, four kids, career twists and turns for both of us, and the daily events that galvanize our lives, that hasn't happened yet. Something tells me that it never will.

JUDY GRUEN

A BORROWED CHILD

I leaf through the album looking for the picture that has become my favorite. There are so many of him as he grew over the five months he was with us, but one in particular holds the message I need to connect with now. I find a photograph of him in the bathtub; another picture shows him grinning directly into the camera with those beautiful Latino eyes. And finally I see the image I need—the picture that speaks of an emotional connection to a child on loan from a desperate mother. In this particular photograph, his back is to the camera, and his face is not visible at all. But the body language says it all, as he lays his head on my daughter's shoulder. His black hair and olive skin contrast sharply to my own child's hazel-eyed blond coloring, yet they hold each other like siblings. His infant arms are wrapped around her neck as she faces the camera—grinning with an inner glow of a child feeling the kind of love free from adult confusions.

What the picture doesn't show is the infant's defect—a missing upper lip and palate and malformed nose. What it does show is my eight-year-old daughter to whom the defect could not matter less.

Our journey with this foster child began on a frigid February day when he was handed to me in a mall parking lot. He arrived from Guatemala after a long and tiring journey with an escort. His only possession was a musty backpack smelling of greasy wood smoke, its contents consisting of two stained shirts sized for an infant twice his age. He arrived with no papers and an uncertain future in his own country, which considered his deformities to be an omen of bad luck. "Eddie's" facial malformation was immediately obvious, and the emotional reaction it caused in most who saw him was always clearly written on their own intact faces.

A mother learns much about her family during times of extreme stress. Families rally or they fragment, but deformed foster children will not allow neutrality of emotion. Slowly and awkwardly we formed our bonds with this malnourished, sick nine-week-old who needed tube feedings, numerous doctor visits, and lots of patience. Our thirteen-year-old swallowed his embarrassment at the attention the baby caused, and despite his attempts at macho indifference, found himself bonding. The middle child, serious and scholastic, kept her distance but became Eddie's most vocal spokesperson to the curious public. Katie, our youngest, loved this foreign child as purely and fiercely as if he had been born to her. Upon first seeing him, she scooped him up and held him tightly to her chest, oblivious to the gaping hole that should have been his lip. Her attitude would foretell their relationship, as he was never far from her thoughts or her physical being. My husband resigned himself to even less attention from his stressed and fatigued wife.

The sleepless nights and sense of responsibility I felt toward this child led to weight loss and panic attacks—symptoms of my physical and emotional struggles as I took up Eddie's cause. During the few quiet moments, I wondered about the mother two thousand miles away yearning for her only child. The organization that sponsored Eddie knew so little about the mother that I was free to imagine my own version, and so to me, she became loving and surely desperate to send her baby to an unknown world.

As Eddie grew, we developed our family flow once more, regaining the chaotic balance we once had. The emotional security fence we had built around our little world was no longer intact. It was not possible to be in public without incurring unwanted attention, and I knew I had adapted when I became oblivious to the stares. As our affection for Eddie grew, we became creative about how to shield him from curious onlookers. Inadvertently, we found ourselves judging people based on their reaction toward him.

In the end, thanks to many wonderful people who donated medical expertise, Eddie was whole again. It was time for him to return to the parents who we had received only one letter from during the five months he had been with us. All we could do was pray that he had remained in their hearts. Our days were spent finding just the right items for his suitcase. Baby clothes, toys, and diapers were purchased and packed, but my mother's heart knew that there were only two things we were sending that were of any lasting value—the Spanish-language Bible and our love.

The day we placed Eddie into the arms of the escort inevitably came. During the sleepless nights, hospitalizations, and surgeries, I had longed for my life to regain some normalcy. Now that the time was here, I felt as if my own child were boarding the plane that would put a vast ocean between us. The force of my emotional pain stunned me, and it fought fiercely with my voice of reason. It was weeks before I could physically touch his baby supplies to pack them away.

The children bore the separation according to their personalities. My son rarely spoke of Eddie and shut down his feelings, as is typical of his age group. Julie, the middle child, stated her desire to save her allowance to someday go to Guatemala and find the child now lost to her. My youngest, Katie, routinely sobbed herself to sleep while voicing her concern that he would forget us. I did not have the heart to tell her that she was right. For months afterward, she slept with his picture taped to her headboard, carefully placed so that he was her first and last thought of the day.

The self-discoveries that Eddie brought to our household would eventually be his greatest gift to our family. Through the trying moments and pain of our separation, my spiritual fortitude grew. And so it was that when the chance to join a medical mission trip to Guatemala became available, I was able to find the inner strength to accept.

Six months after Eddie's return, in a crowded basement room of the clinic we were running in Guatemala, I met his parents for the first time. Through an interpreter, we laughed, cried, and touched with a familiarity forged by the bond of loving the same child. The concern they had for the baby sleeping in their arms was obvious, and I knew now that my heart would be free of the troublesome worries about his circumstances. Thousands of miles from home, in the midst of a roomful of sick children and desperate parents, I sensed the forceful spirit of universal human connection. I had entered this experience thinking of myself as a provider, but now knew that I was but a witness. I was merely a facilitator in the master plan for this child's life, and a grateful observer to the power of a higher being.

JODY GREENLEE

HAVE A LITTLE FAITH

*F*rom *the moment I decided that boys had more to offer than* Matchbox cars and kickball games, I was eager to have a boyfriend. My eagerness, resembling neediness at times, landed me in a series of shallow, empty relationships. Intuitively I thought that I'd know my perfect mate, but I never seemed to listen. Instead, each time I started a new relationship, I'd convince myself that this was "the one."

That all changed when in the summer a couple of years back, I took a weekend trip to Denver for a martial arts festival. My friends and I were sitting in a park watching senior martial arts students test to the next level. I was soaking in all the green around me that was a nice change from the brown, thirsty landscape of Phoenix where I was currently living. Everything about my surroundings appealed to me at that moment, and I thought, *I could live here.* Immediately the hair on my arms and neck stiffened. I felt excited and scared. The more I thought about it the more it seemed like a really good idea. I had no ties in Phoenix. I'd recently ended a ten-year relationship and was feeling restless in my job. Studying Chinese Shaolin Kung Fu had become a significant part of my life, and if I moved to Denver, I could study under the masters who taught there.

Later that day, my friends and I came back to the park to drop off our instructor. A man with a long golden ponytail wearing a black gi caught my attention. He turned around and just like in the movies everything slowed. Our eyes met and my chest tightened. The blood rushed to my head leaving me dizzy. He was handsome, but it was more than that. I *knew* him from somewhere. I recognized something about his eyes.

Without looking away, I elbowed my friend next to me and asked, "Who is that?"

"Oh, that's John Halley," replied my friend. "He has quite a fan club." His tone grew serious. "From what I know of him, he's not really a relationship kind of guy, so you might be better off admiring him from a distance. Like my girlfriend is doing right now."

Over the next two days I kept my eye on John Halley. The dizzy feeling didn't leave me. I couldn't concentrate on the material I was studying. I couldn't hold a conversation. I couldn't eat. I was gone. I noticed that John kept his eye on me, too. Only I couldn't tell if he was looking at me because I was looking at him, or if he was attracted to me as well. We exchanged a few words here and there. He felt *so* familiar. I toyed with the idea of giving him my phone number, but decided against it. I didn't want him to think I was another member of his fan club . . . even though I definitely was one. *This time,* I told myself, *you're going to wait.*

At the end of the weekend, John approached me to say he was planning a trip out west in the fall to visit all of the Shaolin schools in our system and surf the California coast. I told him I could show him around Phoenix if he liked, and he seemed okay with that idea.

On the drive back to Phoenix my head was spinning. Not only did I fall in love with Denver, I was seriously wondering if I'd fallen in love with the mysterious kung fu surfer guy who also happened to live in Denver. I felt confused. How could I feel so strongly about someone I didn't know?

Suddenly, I remembered the reason why John seemed so familiar to me! Five months earlier he had appeared in one of my dreams. He was so vivid in my dream that I recorded it in my dream journal the next morning. Recalling this filled me with even more excitement. *This had to mean something,* I thought. It felt as if my life was about to change.

John was on my mind a lot during the next several months, and I wondered if he thought about me. My daily mantra became "have a little faith."

September came and I found myself looking for John each time I took a class at the kung fu school. But weeks turned into months and I doubted if he was still going to visit our school. With each day that passed, I began to second-guess my experience in Denver. Maybe the whole thing was a product of my sometimes adolescent imagination.

I walked into school in mid-November and saw that familiar mane of golden hair. John was standing at the front desk talking to our instructor. Thousands of butterflies attacked my stomach. I sat down on a bench and took my shoes off, waiting for him to turn around and see me. I must have taken my shoes off and put them back on three times before he finally turned around.

He walked over and asked, "Wendy, right?"

I smiled, trying to keep my cool. "Yeah. And you're John Halley from Denver."

John said he'd been sleeping in his truck for the last two weeks while exploring surf spots in California. I invited him to stay at my house while he was in Phoenix and he accepted. Each time I opened my mouth, I felt more flustered. I was so nervous and excited I could hardly contain myself. Somehow I got through class without getting my teeth kicked in that day.

Afterward, John and I went to a Mexican restaurant. Sitting across from him in the booth, I kept thinking how strange it all was. I could not believe he was right in front of me. I was trying hard to act as if I hadn't spent months thinking about him.

After a few minutes of polite conversation, John said, "I might be making a fool of myself, but I have to ask you something."

I stopped breathing.

"Did something pass between us in Denver?" he asked.

My heart exploded. *I was right! Our experience in Denver had been for real.*

He smiled and said, "I literally felt a jolt when I saw you in Denver. It took me by surprise because I've never had that feeling before. I've thought about you a lot since then and am very curious about what it all means."

"I had the same experience, John, and I haven't been quite the same either. You know, I had a dream about you months before I went to Denver, and I remembered it while I was driving back to Phoenix. Your eyes looked so familiar to me—just like in my dream."

The next two days were the most intense of my life. Being with John felt more like a reunion than a first meeting. We spent the time finding out how oddly perfect we were for each other, both amazed with how much we had in common. It was as if John were the male version of me and I were the female version of him. The more we got to know each other the more everything in my life started making sense. It struck me that our meeting couldn't have been more perfectly orchestrated. We agreed that had we met sooner we wouldn't have been ready for each other.

Little did I know while sitting in the park that July afternoon in Denver that my life truly was about to change forever. I moved to Denver less than a year later, and John *is* okay with being a "relationship kind of guy." We married shortly thereafter.

In the past, I put tremendous energy into trying to force things to happen. I became an expert at making my life more difficult than it needed to be. What was missing was faith. For the first time, I waited for events to unfold after I met John. I decided to trust what was meant to be—and by so doing, I learned that good things come to those who wait.

WENDY STOFAN HALLEY

Courage doesn't always roar. Sometimes courage is the quiet voice
at the end of the day saying, "I will try again tomorrow."
MARY ANNE RADMACHER-HERSHEY

HIS HAND AT MY ELBOW

Many years ago my husband Harry returned home late from a business trip. It was St. Valentine's Day, and as he sheepishly handed me a card, he laughed and said, "Let me be the first to wish you a happy St. Patrick's Day."

He had arrived so late, the drugstore had sold out of valentines. The card he substituted had no shamrocks or leprechauns on the front, just an enormous jolly green giant.

During a marriage that spanned forty-five years, Harry was frequently the jokester, and our time together was enriched by his sense of humor and keen sense of fun.

He died six months ago. When people ask how I am doing, I still reply, "I have lost my rhythm."

I snack instead of cook; I eat in the den rather than at the kitchen table. I miss my sounding board, so I talk to myself and remind myself to tell him something I heard or saw.

The realization that I am alone often overwhelms me. I awoke at two o'clock the other morning devastated by a sense of loss. As I lay there, I recalled that the previous night I had met friends for dinner. When I left the restaurant alone I yearned for my escort. A gentleman of the old school, his hand was always at my elbow. He walked in the rain after depositing me at our destination, parked the car, opened doors, and never preceded me through them.

Tears come often and flow freely. It does not have to be a favorite tune; any romantic rendition on the radio evokes memories. He was a choir member so any hymn sung or played at church makes me weep.

I do dumb things. I let the battery in one car die, neglected an inspection, then had to have "the works." Now that I'm in charge of the tasks he formerly did, I'm aware of the many things I don't know how to do. I watched the captions for the hearing-impaired on my television set for days because I did not know how to remove them. I found myself sighing when the prompter said sigh and giggling when it told me to giggle.

Technology is not my forte, nor am I mechanically inclined. And for many months I could not make a decision. I would ask my yard helper his opinion on inconsequential things: Should a shrub be cut down or the lawn chairs brought in for the winter?

I have experienced the change of three seasons since being alone. In January we had a snowstorm that left us without electricity for days. They were cold and bleak nights. With the arrival of spring I missed my garden cohort. He was the planter; I was the cleaner and raker. But as each blossom appeared I rejoiced at Harry's handiwork.

Now that it is summer, I make beach plans alone.

There's no one to clasp my necklaces, nor does anyone answer when I ask, "How do I look?"

When I told a friend how difficult mornings are, she agreed, "No one likes to get up to an empty house." No one likes to come home to an empty one, either.

Business decisions are mine alone to make. Yesterday my daughter accompanied me when I traded in both cars and leased a new one.

"Dad would've been proud of you," she said. My children and I remember his way of doing things and laugh at our obvious inheritance of the same attitudes and expressions.

I've become proficient at picking up the check, figuring the tip, and paying bills and taxes. The stock market is another story, but I am learning. I've made other strides. I planted a vegetable garden in the plot that was formerly our grandchildren's sandbox. I made a water garden in my backyard. Constantly reminding myself of how much Harry loved life, I have continued social, church, and civic responsibilities. His optimism was contagious; I even talk to all the telemarketers and call them by name as he loved to do. And I am not afraid to stay alone in my house.

On the six-month anniversary of Harry's death, there was a poignant reminder of him. When I went out early to get the paper, I saw the first bloom on a gardenia bush he planted. Earlier in the spring, the pink perfection camellia, which he'd carefully grafted from a neighbor's plant, was a profusion of blossoms for the first time.

I know that Harry is still watching over me because last week a moon vine bloomed at our front door. The seeds were planted in the backyard.

Next year holds more than the promise of daffodils in the spring. We are planting a meditation garden at our church in Harry's memory.

COS BARNES

VII
A POSITIVE POWER SURGE

If you asked me what I came into this world to do,

I will tell you: I came to live out loud.

ÉMILE ZOLA

IRISH TO THE BONE

During the fifteen years I worked in New York City, I avoided going into town on St. Patrick's Day.

"Terrific holiday," I grumped. "Twenty thousand drunk high school kids vomiting in the streets. Anyway, I'm not Irish."

"Hard to believe," my ethnicity-conscious New York friends replied, "you look Irish."

I was sure of my lineage: My mother's ancestry was German, except for a stray French great-grandmother, and Johnny Robertson, my birth father, who was killed in the Second World War, was born of a Scot and his Pennsylvania Dutch wife, Ethel. Ethel Robertson was a mean-spirited woman. She didn't simply have mean thoughts—she wrote them down. Even now, thirty years after her death, many of her vicious letters remain.

Throughout her life, she proudly proclaimed her Pennsylvania Dutch heritage and was contemptuous of more recent immigrants. She was also religiously intolerant, but as she never attended church, exactly which brand of Protestantism she so fervently protected was a mystery.

"My church is the church of the trees and the woods," she would say loftily, although she never, in any of our memories, went into the woods.

In the early nineties, in an effort to reacquaint myself with my long-lost Robertson relations, I visited my father's only surviving brother, my aging and ill uncle Andy. Our conversation drifted to a discussion of my grandmother Ethel.

"My mother was so mean," he said, "that when she died, I stuffed her things into boxes and put them in the attic. I couldn't bear to look at them. Would you be interested in seeing what's there?"

There were pictures, linens, scrapbooks, and hundreds of letters, including a flattened, yellowed bunch secured with a pink ribbon. Sitting with my uncle, side by side in leather recliners, I untied the ribbon and began to read the first letter, and then the second. They were my grandparents' love letters, written between 1911 and 1913, when they were engaged. My grandfather, twenty, was in college in his home state of Ohio, and my grandmother, seventeen, was finishing high school in Pennsylvania.

Declaring her eternal love in perfect Palmer penmanship, my grandmother wrote: "For you, my darling Scotsman, I will leave my beloved church and cloak my beloved father's history. I will turn my back on the nuns and the priests who have been my solace and my inspiration, and I will deny my Irish blood. As it says in the Book of Ruth, for the love of you, your people will become my people and your God, my God." I was reading aloud to my uncle. " 'Today, I have made my last confession in the Roman church.' "

I was stunned, recalling my grandmother's appalling prejudices.

"Rocha," she repeated carefully upon meeting a high school boyfriend of mine. "What kind of a name is that?"

"Portuguese," he said, timidly.

"Are you a Catholic, then, my dear?" she pronounced each word like Dracula intoning, "I-don't-drink-wine."

"Did you know this, Uncle Andy? Did you know this?"

Tears were streaking my uncle's pale cheeks. "I did not know, until now," he said, "that my mother was Irish. I didn't know, until now, that my mother was Catholic. And this is the first time I have ever known that my parents loved each other."

Today, I look in the mirror: Not even wrinkles and gray streaks can completely obscure the red hair and freckles. My bookshelf is filled with the writings of Swift, Yeats, Synge; my music library is modern Irish tunes and Celtic melodies. I am not a Catholic, but I choose—as I have always chosen—to attend a formally liturgical Protestant church. How could I have not suspected?

When, in the course of casual conversations, people would ask me about my national origins, I used to reply that I was the usual American mongrel mix—and I was a bit envious of people who had a strong sense of a specific heritage. No longer. A few days ago, I was asked the question again.

"I'm Irish," I said.

"Oh!" laughed the man who'd inquired, "that explains every-thing."

"Yes," I said, "it does."

WENDY (REID CRISP) LESTINA

Sometimes freedom is worth whatever you have to pay for it.
LINDA NASH

LIVING ALONE

When my grandparents and I immigrated to the United States, I was a shy, fourteen-year-old refugee girl who spoke broken English and took refuge in the books at the library. We lived in an ethnic neighborhood in the city, in a house with no yards to speak of. But in the books I sought out, I could wander around in the country with heroines like Eleanora, in my favorite book, *Girl of the Limberlost,* or Anne of the *Anne of Green Gables* tales. Those books transported me to beautiful green settings where my youthful yearnings could be let loose with the heroines of the tales. And I vowed to myself that one day those beautiful green surroundings would be mine for real.

When I married in the late fifties, I went from living at home with my gentle, loving grandparents to living with a tyrant. It soon became obvious that nothing I did would ever please him, but I learned to live with it. After all, soon there were three kids to consider, along with a nice new house in the suburbs and winter vacations in Florida as well, so what did it matter that my self-esteem had hit rock bottom?

When I reached middle age and the kids were grown and living lives of their own, I decided enough was enough and filed for a divorce. However, being alone was not something I was prepared for. Neither was working for a living. The divorce settlement included a house and a small income, but it wasn't enough of an income to cover all the expenses of suburban living.

Luckily, I was hired for the first job I applied for. It was a job on the night shift of a Car Parts warehouse, so it wasn't something to brag about, but it would help pay some bills and it was only two miles from home, especially important to someone intimidated by freeway driving.

The first year alone was miserable. Whenever I was home from work, the television was blaring in the living room, while the radio in the kitchen was doing the same. Not that I was watching or listening to either. They were on to fill the vacuum of silence, to give the illusion of someone being with me.

That Christmas, my two sons, who were in the armed services, came home on leave, and my newly married daughter and son-in-law were with me. But on New Year's Eve I was alone, and thought I'd die of loneliness. I remember feeling sorry for myself as I sat in front of the television and thought about all the lucky people celebrating with friends and loved ones. I wanted to be out dancing and laughing and having fun, instead of crying myself to sleep long before the clock struck midnight.

Gradually, though, a sense of self-worth came creeping back into my psyche. "You can do anything you want now," I began telling myself at the nightly pep sessions I held with myself. "You can choose to make the best of things, or you can stay miserable. Figure out what would make you happy, and go for it, woman."

So I made a list of things that would make me happy. Number one on the list was to get a dog or a cat. My ex-spouse didn't approve of pets, so we hadn't had one, but I loved animals.

A few days later, I visited our local Humane Society. A short time later, I was driving home with a young black Lab, whose soulful brown eyes and wagging tail promised many happy days ahead. And in the cat carrier the Humane Society loaned me, two scaredy tabbies were about to get a new home, too. Suddenly there was a black dog to romp with, and two cats to snuggle with, and life wasn't so bad after all.

Then, one Saturday morning, I decided to visit our public library. It had been my favorite haunt in the past, but I had not been there in ten years. I felt like Alice in Wonderland! Browsing happily among the aisles of books I came to one containing books about nature and country living, and felt myself drawn to them like a magnet. I picked out several books and settled in for a weekend of reading. It was wonderful.

Gradually, it dawned on me that it wasn't enough just to read about nature and country living. I wanted to *be* in the country. And the vow I made to myself as a teenager surfaced and I realized it was now or never! So I put the house up for sale soon after, and went searching for my dream.

In retrospect, I realize I jumped into the decision without much thought. However, I did have a small income to rely on and planned to make extra money writing. Writing had been the dream I never had time for while I lived in the city. I also had the money from the sale of my suburban house, which, of course, paid for the property I decided to buy.

Several months were filled with the excitement of searching for my own special country haven. By August 1983, I had sold my house in the city and had a rustic house on nearly a hundred acres in the wilds of the beautiful Ozarks. Some friends, who couldn't believe I would just leave lock, stock, and barrel, tried to change my mind with scary snake stories.

But my kids were happy that I was going after my dream. I, of course, was overjoyed, snakes or no snakes!

Now I live in a house in the woods. My most immediate neighbors are deer, raccoon, opossum, wild turkey, coyote, black bear, the occasional armadillo that's moseyed its way to our parts from Texas, and various and sundry reptiles. I revere all of them. The wilds just wouldn't be the wilds without them.

Of course, there are dogs and cats, and fluffy-as-a-cloud bantam chickens. Several ducks add their quacking to the special country ambiance, too. Who says living alone has to be lonely and miserable? Not me, that's for sure. I have been alone for several years now, and I am doing just fine, thank you. And my three little granddaughters, city girls, get to spend their vacations in the country.

I am so glad I had the fortitude to change my life. The old adage says, "Life is what you make it." I have chosen to make my life joyful and fun. Besides, there is nothing empty about living alone—I have never felt so full.

RENIE SZILAK BURGHARDT

BATTER UP

I *sit looking at the envelope and refuse to hold back the tears as I* remember.

We began as babies. All of us in our late teens and early twenties. All but one, very single and ready for just about anything. None of us had ever played softball on any real team before. Most of us knew each other, but really didn't hang together. It was the dream of one person to put together a team. And so the "dream team" emerged.

Positions were assigned by asking what scared us the least on the field. That was where we played. We lost that first game twenty-something to one. We got killed in the second game by a score we have all tried to forget. And then it happened: We came around. That first victory broke open something inside us that needed letting out. We went on to win the league that year and the end-of-the-year tournament. We dominated the league for the next fourteen years. We were The Truckers.

The phenomenal thing about us was that we stuck together. The team survived weddings and babies, death and divorce. We played through rain and snow. We saw people come and go and yet the core group remained. We grew into a family of our own. And when tragedy hit my family and my brother died, The Truckers were there en masse, donating the tree that stands in his memory in my front yard.

The last five years that we played, we weren't as competitive as the other teams. We believed that the best player for the position was the one who had stuck it out for all those years. The best team member was the one who held your heart when it was obvious that you couldn't let it beat on its own. So as other teams beefed up their lineups, we just beefed up. The games were the reason we came together. The friendships were the reasons we stayed together.

In the last season of play, we had new shirts made with the slogan:

This is it!
Truckers
1975–1995

I tried another team after The Truckers, but it didn't work. We had raised ourselves on sportsmanship and good team spirit: Never yell at the ref—even when he cost us the game. Never slide to take someone out. Never criticize the play of your teammate. Never go home without letting someone know you are leaving.

We were branded by some as a clique. We were feared and dubbed the team everyone would most like to beat. And when the last five years rolled around, we were the team everyone wanted to play—it was a sure win.

So five years after we encircled home plate and celebrated The Truckers' postgame gathering for the last time, Julie called to let me know we would be having a Trucker reunion. I was overjoyed! I missed the carpool ride out to the newly purchased lake home where the reunion was held, but I had the directions. When I arrived later, I was greeted by the friends I had made playing softball.

They told me to put my two dollars into the kitty for the door prize. I have never liked silly games—only real games like softball —so I made some excuse about not having money with me. Promptly, Julie wrote out an IOU, and I was officially in the door-prize drawing. We were asked to relate a favorite memory from the Trucker years and offer a toast for all Truckers. As we went around the table and talked, we laughed and quickly wiped away tears that sprang into our eyes. When my turn finally came I offered this toast; "To the girls I grew up with, and the ladies I will grow old with."

We no sooner had "clinked" our plastic wineglasses and downed the drink when Julie said it was time for the door prize. She asked if I had signed my name on a slip of paper for the door prize. Even though I protested that I had already signed the IOU, they made sure I wrote my name on a slip of paper and put it into the fishbowl with the others. Susie drew out the name and much to my relief I noticed that it was larger than the paper I had written on. I couldn't believe it when Julie read, "Bette."

"Can't be me." I said. "I wrote on a smaller piece of paper. Someone must have put my name in before."

Julie reached in and pulled out the next slip, "Bette," she read. Another slip, "Bette." She continued doing this until all slips were out of the jar and all had "Bette" written on them.

"I guess that means you win the door prize, Bette," Julie said as she handed me a huge manila envelope.

The room had become all too quiet as I carefully fingered the seal and finally ripped it open. Inside was the card. I opened the pale white envelope that held the card and read the thank-you printed on the front. I was just a bit confused when I opened the card and twenty-dollar and ten-dollar bills fell out. The Truckers had written how much they appreciated all that I had done and sacrificed for them as coach for the last several years we were together. Now it was their turn to sacrifice for me.

The money, they said, was earmarked for something special of my choosing. I could not use it to pay bills or buy monthly groceries. Tears, hugs, and silence—only comfortable when shared with friends—filled the room as I promised to find a good use for the money.

Today as I look at the envelope that is filled with hard-earned dollars and love, I am reminded that friends—true friends—always find a way to give of themselves, and that playing sports builds relationships that can't be broken over time.

ELIZABETH KRENIK (TRAXLER)

MOMMY INTELLECTUAL

Ten years out of school and two babies at home—I needed an escape from the *Sesame Street* world where I lived. Thus I found myself in a graduate English course, Images of Women in Literature, during the following fall semester.

I had forgotten how tricky parking on a college campus could be and ran hard to make it to the classroom on time. I huffed in and saw two other women in smart pantsuits, a bearded gentleman in his thirties, and three younger women who had the casual, bored look of college students on the first day of class. They all chatted easily with each other.

I sat down at the other end of the semicircle of desks, feeling conspicuous in my worn denim jumper. I glanced down self-consciously, hoping I didn't smell like baby formula or carry the stains of the macaroni and cheese my toddler liked to toss around the kitchen table.

The professor arrived five minutes after the scheduled time. "Hello! Hello! I'm Dr. Helena Monahan. Please call me Sister Helena. This is Images of Women in Literature. Welcome."

I tried to relax and smile at her, but she pulled out a computer printout and quickly called out names. Mine wasn't on the list.

"I registered—I have a receipt," I told her, lifting up my purse.

"This happens all the time. Just give me your name and I'll write it down," she said, and after that she told everyone, "I'd like you to talk first. Why don't each of you tell me what you've been reading lately?"

I was suddenly nervous. What had I read lately? I had read *Toilet Training Success Stories*. I could recite *The Cat in the Hat,* and I knew every verse to "The Farmer in the Dell." Somehow I knew it wasn't what the others had read lately.

Luckily I was the last one in the semicircle to share. I knew some of the authors the others named, but in my former job as a middle-school English teacher I had concentrated more on grammar and vocabulary than on literature.

What was I doing here among these intellectuals? What had made me believe I could compete with them?

Finally, it was my turn to talk. "Lately, I've read the philosophy of Dr. Seuss, studied with great regularity the classics of children's literature like *Ferdinand the Bull* and *Stone Soup,* and discovered the poetry of limericks and knock-knock jokes."

Only the professor laughed. The others looked at me with blank expressions.

"I'm a stay-at-home-mom for now. I have a nine-month-old and a two-year-old at home. I read a lot of kid's books, you know?"

They nodded at me, but I felt like I had spoken to them in a dead language.

Sister Helena began the evening's lecture, and while the other students seemed to easily make connections between classic and contemporary literature, I realized that my undergraduate English courses had left me with name recognition but no real depth of knowledge. I didn't take notes as fast as the others did, and many of the women authors in the professor's lecture were unfamiliar to me.

What was I doing here? I barely heard the professor going over the schedule of reading, notification of two ten-page research papers, and a final project. She asked all of us to read Henry James's *Portrait of a Lady* by the next class meeting. I heard someone murmuring about 350 pages. In seven days?

Did this professor know that a mom with two babies couldn't even go to the bathroom without a captive audience? I dropped into bed exhausted every night. Where was I supposed to find time to read 350 pages?

Everyone filed out of the classroom. Some of them talked about meeting for coffee later to discuss the reading list. I felt so alien to these graduate students. I didn't belong.

"Diane? It's Diane, right?"

It took me a second to realize Dr. Monahan was talking to me.

"Yes—hi—doctor—professor—Sister." I was a jumbled mess.

"I can tell by your face, Diane. You want to drop this class, don't you?"

Was she psychic? No, just a nun. And after all my Catholic schooling, it shouldn't have surprised me. You can't hide anything from a nun.

"I—I don't think I belong here," I said, thinking of the graduate English program.

She reached out and clasped my arm. "Diane, don't let this class intimidate you. You'll do just fine in here." She gave me an earnest smile. "I can tell that you're having second thoughts. Don't give up. I want you in my class."

Her words were like a hug from Mommy and a kiss for a boo-boo.

"You're right, Sister. I'm having second thoughts. Everyone else is so well read. They're intellectuals."

"But they haven't lived the life you have, Diane. Do you realize how much your experiences as a mom will add to the class discussions?"

I raised my eyebrows at her question, and she laughed.

"Don't you see? The theme of the course is Images of Women in Literature. Motherhood is one of the major roles for women."

I knew she was right, and smiled at Sister Helena.

"I'll be here next week," I promised. "You can count on me."

I was surprised by my determination to give up afternoon soap operas and read while the kids napped. I convinced my husband to push the stroller after supper, and asked my mother-in-law to stay with the children on two afternoons so I could read for college at the library.

That week my house wasn't very clean, but I had managed to read the book. I walked into the class, ready to share my ideas and insights into one author's work. I sat beside one of the younger girls and asked, "What did you think of the novel?"

"Oh, I only got to page fifty," she said. "I had things to do last week."

I recalled everything I had done during the past week, as well as the many tasks I finished just before class so I could get away for a few hours. Plus I read 350 pages.

When the professor arrived and we started class discussion, it took only a few minutes to realize that I was the only one who had completed the assignment. That's when I truly felt proud of myself and knew I could compete with these other graduate students as a Mommy Intellectual.

Sister Helena was right. I had a lot to contribute in graduate classes, and earned my degree three years later. And because of her, I now sit in the college professor's chair and carefully look around during that first class in English composition. I want to see which new students might need those extra words of encouragement to stay in college and succeed on their own terms.

DIANE GONZALES BERTRAND

People with good intentions never give up!
JANE SMILEY

ONE STEP AT A TIME

My husband has always had many great and practical ideas, but I really began to wonder about him the day he came home and said, "How about we build a kit home?"

My knowledge of building was limited, but I did at least know what a kit home was. A lot of prefabricated frames bolted together, covered with some sort of cladding with wood on the outside and plaster on the inside. But even my simplistic view of the construction did nothing to improve my confidence in us building one.

Up until that day, my husband, Steve, and I had done very little work around our small apartment other than the standard painting of walls and hanging pictures. Of course, there had been the small shelf we had put up in the kitchen for the toaster. The shelf lasted a week before it fell down with a terrifying crash in the middle of the night, scaring us both half to death.

I had always thought that kit homes were for those who knew about building, or at least knew about basic household projects. After all, this was a house we were talking about. A house! Four walls, one roof, somewhere supposedly safe to live. Not just a picturesque mailbox that held little danger to anyone, or anything, should it collapse in a halfhearted breeze.

During the weeks that followed, my head swarmed with nightmares of collapsing walls, flyaway rooftops, and doors that didn't fit into door frames. This vision of a crooked, ramshackle house was certainly not the kind of a place that I had planned to bring up our children.

For months I tried to ignore Steve's interest in the project. *He'll get tired of it,* I thought. Ignore the idea and it'll go away. It must! But it didn't. Steve stayed as keen as ever.

Eventually, I couldn't ignore the suggestion any longer. I decided if only for peace and quiet to go with him and visit a few showrooms. As I stood there, a flesh statue of negativity, I listened to the salesman's spiel, amazed by how easy he made the building sound. "Our houses are designed for everyday people," he said. "The directions are easily read and understood. If you have any problems we will always be around to help you out." I must admit that my intrigue increased as I thought about the money we would save by building over buying an established house.

In the end, I agreed to go ahead with it, although still at the back of my mind raged that one nagging doubt: How could we, who couldn't fix a shelf, build a house? The task seemed so huge that, despite my excitement at starting a new adventure, I suffered from even more nightmares than before. What if we hurt ourselves putting everything together? How will we know which way up to put the windows? Heck, I don't even know how to use a drill! As the days lessened before the house framework would arrive, my questions increased. But my husband stayed focused on his vision of building our dream home.

When the truck finally pulled into our new driveway, I just stood and stared. Tears stung my eyes as the enormity of the task ahead hit home. Still, as the salesman had said, we did have our manual to refer to and there was help on the other end of the phone if we needed it. So, bright and early the next morning, we were down on our block of land, standing by the concrete pad, reading the manual.

Step 1: Place steel frames on the ground next to where they have to stand.

Well, that sounds pretty straightforward, I thought. And, to my surprise, it was.

Step 2: Bolt all the steel frames together to create the house framework.

Once again, this was easily done, and we went on by putting one foot in front of the other.

Of course, a lot of delays and interesting moments requiring our brain power evolved, yet many humorous moments compensated for them. Challenges such as how to get the central beam that ran the length of the house up onto the steel framework so that we could rest the roof on it. Not easy when our combined strength could only carry the wooden beam.

Then there was the night when after two days of dawn-to-dusk tiling I bolted upright in bed and attempted to tile the bed while still asleep. When we tried to fix a series of ten-foot-long plasterboard sheets in our ceiling, even a square foot of the material was too heavy for either of us to hold over our heads for any length of time. Yet we overcame all of these challenges by ourselves with a little bit of thought, ingenuity, and patience. Not once did we find ourselves calling the salesman for help.

The memorable day finally arrived when we stood back and looked proudly at our completed home. The home we had built by ourselves. Our house looked so immovable and solid with its straight walls and squared door frames, a secure roof, and well-placed plug holes. A home that I knew was more than safe in which to bring up a family.

I marveled at all we had learned in the last twelve months. I marveled at our abilities and resourcefulness. Even more, I marveled at my husband's confidence in our joint capabilities. Standing there that day, both relieved and in awe of the finished product, I realized something profound. Something that, no doubt, many people facing the odds had realized before me.

Whenever I am faced with a task that seems insurmountable, even that which looks impossible, with faith and determination all I need do is just take one step at a time. A Chinese proverb says it this way: "The man who removes a mountain begins by carrying away small stones."

ELIZABETH BEZANT

DOOR NUMBER FOUR

"*Has it kicked in yet?*" *my friend asked.*

"Do you mean my life or the Prozac?" I responded.

My friend and I were discussing my latest brilliant attempt to rid myself of my-life-is-over, empty-nest-induced depression. Six months earlier, my only child had left home for college, and my heart followed in search of a Band-Aid. I had scanned bookstore shelves for self-help books on finding yourself, listened to 2:00 A.M. infomercials tell me how to find contentment in my life, and wolfed down vitamins, herbs, and supplements all designed to boost my pleasure principle. Finally, with no relief in sight, I abandoned self-remedies and visited Dr. Feel Good, who determined I demonstrated the required condition for medication. He suggested something to get me over the hump.

"Doc, this is a mountain, not a hump."

The prescription for tinkering with my gears was Prozac. I hesitated, concerned that these miracle pills would change me into someone else, but I realized I had long since ceased to recognize myself anyhow. Even if these mood enhancers fell short of producing the old me (not exactly a lofty goal in itself), anything was better than the present me. However, due to the chemical reaction of Prozac in the brain, everyone responds differently and results may not appear for six weeks or more. I was in the fourth week waiting for the old me, the new me, or anyone else who dared show up.

Later that same day, I went to the drugstore to have my prescribed salvation refilled, hoping the second month's supply would kick in and bring me home. Expressing words of encouragement, the pharmacist, who was also a friend, handed me my transportation to redemption: However, he did not release his grip on the bag.

"You know, Paula, maybe you don't need this; maybe what you need is a life."

Just what I needed—more advice, something I was not lacking during this period of my life. Solicited or not, everyone had an opinion regarding what I should be doing. I felt like a contestant on *Let's Make a Deal* and Monty Hall was presenting doors for me to choose from: "Paula, let's make a deal; you can keep your life or you can trade it for what's behind the first door; show Paula what's behind door number one! . . . It's tennis every day with the girls, followed by lunch at the country club and afternoon shopping!"

My husband was encouraging me, "Yeah, Paula, pick that door! That's just what you need!"

"What else ya got, Monty?"

"You're going to love this, Paula! Show Paula door number two! . . . It's a social butterfly! You'll organize fundraisers, give luncheons for the committees at your home, and attend every charity ball in town!"

"Maybe you better show me something else."

"Paula, you're running out of doors here. Show Paula door number three! . . . We have a lady of leisure! You'll sleep the morning away, rent movies for the afternoon, putter in your garden, accompanied by a year's supply of Prozac!"

"Gee, Monty, I think I'll just keep my life and go home; besides, I'm kinda getting the hang of this whole self-pity thing."

Frankly, I wouldn't have recognized a good deal if it had dressed itself up in its Sunday best and rung my doorbell. I felt useless, worthless, and joyless. When I wasn't filling my thoughts with self-loathing, something kept gnawing at me—something that had chewed at my conscience many times over the years: All my adult life I regretted not going to college.

Shortly after getting married, I applied to school, but my husband expressed discontent with the idea. He had waited a long time to get married and craved home-cooked meals, an orderly house, and a partner to help him achieve his career goals. (Where was Gloria Steinem when I needed her?) To be honest, my husband didn't exactly have to twist my arm; I relented without much of a struggle. When my son was born, I didn't want to miss a moment of being a mother, so college was easily forgotten—well, not completely forgotten. I would be rudely reminded now and then in social situations when someone would ask. "So, Paula, where did you go to school?" The first time I gave the name of my high school until I got the hang of it and became an expert on having near-deaf experiences.

I finally realized (with a little help from my friendly pharmacist-turned-counselor) I didn't need my Prozac refilled, I needed a trip to the college admissions office. After leaving the drugstore, I went home and made the appointment. Once I'd made the decision to go to college and had been accepted, I finally told my husband. Initially, I mentioned taking just *one* class. Gradually I worked up enough bravado to say *full-time* to my husband.

"What do you mean full-time?" he asked.

"It means you'll be taking your own shirts to the laundry and dinner will be every man for himself." (Gloria would be proud.)

There was a very long silence until finally a smile started across my husband's face; he gave me a hug and said, "You go get 'em, Paula."

I didn't sleep for weeks before my first day of class. Admittedly, I was in doubt whether I could keep up with students young enough to be my children, and whether I really wanted to devote the next few years of my life to lectures instead of liposuction, studying instead of shopping, and psychology exams instead of psychologist appointments. At least I didn't have to worry about sorority rush, getting a date for homecoming, and bulimic roommates.

I started that summer and did take just one class to familiarize myself with the campus, but in the fall I was a full-time student. The first day I attended class I *knew* I had made the right decision. I remember walking out of class that day and breathing in a new, exciting, Prozac-free life.

I never thought I would be carrying around bifocals, Doan's pills, and Preparation H in my book bag when I finally got to make this journey, but it's better than not taking the trip. That's not to say the road wasn't a little bumpy at first. I knew I was way over that hump when my son called one Sunday morning from school to tell me he was coming home for the day, and I asked, "Why?"

He laughed and said, "You've come a long way, Mother. A year ago if I had said I was coming home, you would have cried and then fussed over me all day."

"Well," I said, "I've given up the crying, but I can't make any promises about the fussing."

After my son's call I sat down at my desk, anxious to squeeze in a little studying before my son arrived home, and realized joy had returned to my life along with self-worth and a feeling of accomplishment. Most important, *I* had returned—not a new me, not a fabricated me, but an improved old me. The depression that accompanied my empty-nest syndrome had been replaced by my goal of becoming a college graduate. That goal also became graduating with a straight-A average. Three and a half years after starting my journey, I received my diploma with honors.

The next time I saw Dr. Feel Good, he inquired, "I noticed you haven't been refilling your Prozac, Paula. How's that mountain?"

"I climbed it," I answered, holding up my charm bracelet so that he could see my Phi Beta Kappa key dangling from my wrist.

PAULA CONRAD MLEKUSH

MINDFUL GARDENING

"You have cancer," the doctor in his crisp white coat said.

Stunned and shaken, feeling like I was in the middle of a seven-point earthquake, I did what any other self-respecting holistic healing person would do. I stepped out of my body. Stopped breathing. *Did he just say the C word? Maybe he has the wrong Judith Fraser. Wrong report. In a second, he'll notice his mistake, and it will all just be another glitch in my past.*

"What's my next step?" I asked. My voice a faroff echo.

"A CAT scan or an MRI," he said.

Damn, my dream was right. That dream I'd had last week: I was on an ocean ship. I tried to save a cat perched on the edge of a railing. And failed. The cat bit me on the back of the neck.

I had many such dreams in the next week as I prepared for surgery. In one, I found a large pool of water with a guitar case submerged in the middle. I fretted that the guitar inside would be ruined. The delicate strings and smooth casing would no longer be able to send music into the world. Over to one side of the pool was a broken pot, filled with small flowers. I worried that the flowers would die. They were no longer safely contained.

"The cancer in your uterus was unusual," the doctor announced after surgery. "It could have grown anywhere in your body. You were fortunate that it grew in an area that is protected."

"We are running tests on some of your lymph nodes to see if you'll need chemotherapy or radiation," he said.

The dreams continued. One night, my husband and I were riding bicycles. A large mudhole on our path blocked easy access to the rental shed. The owner told us to take the oceanfront route, where we'd have to dodge some scattered gunfire, then return the bicycles at the next shed.

"You will need six weeks of radiation," the doctor said on my return visit. "Several lymph nodes came back positive."

"Is radiation something like gunfire?" I asked, grateful for the angels who forewarned me through my dreams.

As a therapist, I knew most people had a tough time facing their mortality. With cancer placing my own mortality in question, the scale was now tipped in death's favor in the daily roundabout of death chasing life. That finely calibrated line between the two sharpened my daily focus. I was keenly aware of exactly what *is* important.

"What alternative treatments have helped in cases like mine?" I asked.

"I don't know," he said.

When I got home, I pulled out my colored pencils and drew my illness. Carefully I layered it with the colored rays of the Sun and Earth. I closed my eyes and entered the garden inside my body. The images told me it needed help. I hired a full-time "gardener" and added herbs and teas to my nutrition list.

I couldn't help but think: if I died who would remind my kids of the most important things in life? And who would walk in my space, hear the wise words of my friends, and celebrate their success? Who would share the ups and downs of my clients in their journey toward expanded awareness? Who would be there grinning ear to ear when my son opens his new restaurant? Who would be down front and center to applaud my daughter's next show? Who will rock my grandchildren to sleep and sing them songs my grandmother sang to me? Who will sit with my husband on the front swing and watch the hummingbirds dip their fragile beaks into the sweetness of our bright orange blossoms?

Over the weeks, friends visited, sent flowers, mailed charming or funny cards, put me on their prayer lists, sent tapes, shopped,

and cooked for my family and me. I thought about finding a sur-
rogate wife for my husband, but he wouldn't have anything to do
with it.

There's a list on my fridge now, next to the magnetic poetry my
daughter gave me. It has names and numbers of people willing to
drive me to the hospital when the radiation makes me too tired to
go on my own.

During my next visit I said to my doctor, "I've learned of one
alternative treatment that helps. Love, of life and each other."

JUDITH MORTON FRASER

The only courage that matters
is the kind that gets you from one moment to the next.
MIGNON MCLAUGHLIN

HUMMINGBIRD SUMMER

Some of my favorite childhood memories center on my grandmother's yard, which was graced with two gigantic mimosa trees. In the spring and summer, the trees, with their sweeping limbs and fluffy, sweet-smelling pink flowers, were havens for hummingbirds. It seemed like thousands of the minute, fairylike creatures filled the branches. It was a sight I never tired of, and I spent hours watching them. Fascinated with their whirring wings, I tried to get close enough to the little birds to study them. They were too shy to let me get near, though, and I had to be content with watching from a distance.

Then I grew up and moved away. Years passed and I saw fewer and fewer hummingbirds. Sometimes I would spot one while visiting friends who had flower gardens, but the sightings were few and far between. Then something happened to make me wonder if anything in my life would ever be as simple or as innocent as watching hummingbirds again.

My marriage, troubled from the beginning, had collapsed and I barely escaped with my life. Bruised in body and spirit, I fled to a domestic violence shelter. I had always been a private person, and having to live in this new place, filled with other women trying to make sense of the same sorts of horrible things that had happened to me, was almost more than I could bear. My heart cried out for privacy, for time to heal, and for the assurance that things would be all right again. Though I was physically safe, I had doubts that my mind or my soul would ever heal. It was as though I had lost everything, even myself.

The shelter staff was compassionate and understanding. They assured me that I could stay as long as I needed. They even gave me a job, which, in turn, helped reassure me that I hadn't lost everything; I could still type, file, and do any office work they needed. Each skill remembered was a tiny step forward.

My abuse had been so severe, the police felt it was better for me to stay in the shelter as long as possible. Threats had been made against my life and I would be safer there. But I was beginning to feel stifled and as I grew stronger, I needed a space of my own; I craved a place where I could begin to stand on my own two feet and to regain my independence. That's when my family stepped in.

They moved an old mobile home to a spot near my dad's place and fixed it up for me. My father planted a pear tree and several strong young oaks in the yard. My sister-in-law created a small flowerbed, and other family members pitched in to do some yard work and make minor repairs to the trailer. It was a cute little place, and I was happy to settle into it. With family living on each side of me, I had a secure, albeit very old, home. Still suffering nightmares and flashbacks of the abuse, my nerves were still stretched wire-thin, though, and every noise or sudden movement startled me. Warily, I set out on the journey to a new life.

One day my dad tapped on my door. I opened it to find him standing there, clutching several red and white plastic objects. "Here," he said, thrusting them into my hands. "I thought you might like these."

Surprised, I realized that the funny red and white things were my mom's old hummingbird feeders. They were dirty and scuffed up, but they looked usable. A twinge of something nudged my heart. Suddenly, I found myself transported back through the years to my grandma's yard. Could some of those funny, swift-flying little birds still be around? A glimmer of excitement, of timid anticipation, took hold.

I cleaned the feeders with boiling water and a brush, then filled them with sugar water. Carefully, I hung them on a length of clothesline stretched between two porch supports. Before long, I was rewarded with the sight of a tiny, shimmering body buzzing around one of the feeders. It hovered there, sipped from one of the feeder ports, then zoomed away. Later that day, a couple more tiny diners paid my outdoor café a visit. A little bit of warmth crept into the dark, cold recess that filled my heart. For the first time in a long while, I looked forward to something.

The summer wore on and eventually, I found myself growing stronger. It was an agonizingly slow process, and I had many setbacks. Sometimes it seemed for every step forward, I fell back two. Yet something inside, some stubborn part of myself that I'd thought buried, kept driving me to put one foot in front of the other, to take each day one difficult moment at a time.

On really bad days, I would sit quietly on my porch and watch the hummingbirds. While they appeared fragile, they were strong. Though they were tiny, nothing intimidated them. And they were incredibly active, yet took time to hover in place at the feeders and enjoy the nectar that nourished them. It occurred to me to try standing still, to hover in place, and to find nourishment in the simple passage of time.

I learned many lessons that summer. I learned that moving forward didn't come in giant leaps; rather, it took many tiny, tentative steps. I learned that healing could not be rushed and that there was more strength inside me then I ever realized. I learned that if I sat very still, I could hear a small voice inside telling me that I was worthwhile, that I was somebody, and that I would reclaim my life. I learned not to give up. And gradually I learned the way back to myself.

ANNE CULBREATH WATKINS

MAINTAINING THE BLOOM

*I*made an investment the other day. Something, I thought, to champion self-esteem, a purchase to aid farsighted eyes. I invested
in a high-tech, highly magnified, wall-mounted mirror.

Self-esteem? Aid for farsighted eyes?

Take my pores. Magnified five times they seemed big enough
to swim in. And the long and short marks I discovered on my
nose—broken capillaries, not Morse code.

Need I mention wrinkles—the hours spent in youthful obliv-
ion, flip-flopping my body in the sun till I reached the reddened
hue of plums? Why now was I shocked to see that plums dry to
prunes?

One friend, who was once a plum, suggested I see her aesthetician, a fancy name for someone who reaps joy over the prospect
of selling hundreds of dollars of skin care products to rehabbed
sun worshippers.

My initial visit was humbling. Reclining on a padded table, I allowed Jennifer the aesthetician to strip my face down to the skin
and bare lashes. I was weak-kneed from loss of makeup when she
propped me against a pitted, white wall and, at close range, shot
me with a Polaroid. That's when I grasped the nitty-gritty of envi-
ronmentally damaged skin, and how bad I looked in a shower cap.

Back on the table, Jennifer scrutinized my face behind a disc-
shaped glass loaded with magnification. She looked like a Cyclops
in tortoiseshell frames. I squeezed my eyes shut as she probed, lec-
tured, extracted, and swabbed.

On final analysis I received a D for sun exposure, but gained
new vocabulary: hyperpigmentation, antioxidants, free radicals,

laser resurfacing, Retinol, and dermaplaning—a process in which a scalpel is scraped across the face to remove dead skin cells. It gives new meaning to a close shave.

I drove home with five frilly pink bags filled with skin-plumping activators, clarifying emulsions, and emu extract—purchases that left me four hundred dollars poorer. And I thought, maybe it's time to fess up and admit defeat. So what if your lipstick bleeds into tiny lines? Look yourself in your 5 × mirror and face maturity with maturity. Then I thought, maybe I'll grow a mustache.

A nightly regimen of slathering facial products demands discipline. Each application requires a drying period, which begets another application. This goes on for hours till my arms burn and the muscles pump, but it saves me a workout at the gym.

I begin with a cleanser crammed with benefits such as hydrolyzed oat flour. I let it dry. Then I spray my face with a toner made with castor oil. I let it dry and watch CNN. The facial lotion process takes me through Leno, and the slow-prep Retinol cream through the late show and the late, late show. Next, I apply the emu extract. It contains no oat flour, but does have the rich, gelatinous properties of my grandmother's chicken schmaltz.

Some nights I apply a green sulfurous cream, which promotes tighter pores. It hardens into a mask. It smells. But that's not the worst of it. The clinging aroma of rotten eggs sends my husband into the outstretched arms of our sofa.

Jennifer, my aesthetician, suggested I trade my mirror for a more realistic view. I say no. For wasn't it once said, "You can never be too rich or too young-looking" . . . or maybe the quote is "too rich or too thin"? Regardless, I'd settle for one of them.

SHELLEY SIGMAN

VIII
FAMILY MATTERS

Plan to be surprised. That's my motto.

SUSAN SARANDON

OUT OF SYNC

The toddlers in our playgroup rushed eagerly to their smiling mothers, hands in the air, fingers at the ready. They bounced with anticipation: Would it be Itsy-Bitsy Spider this time? Or the Pooh game?

Only I sat alone: My twenty-month-old toddler was busy jamming compact discs into the CD player, one after the other. I waited, resigned to what would surely happen next.

"Well, he knows what he wants!" one young mother smiled nervously. "Is it the Barney song? Or Elmo?"

You wish, I wanted to say, but time had run out. The sudden thunder of synthesizers and metal guitars and keyboards jolted everyone. One boy burst into tears. Others clung to their mothers in confusion. My son, of course, danced with delight. I would have run from the house in embarrassment. Except that it was my house.

"Ummm, what is that?" A few tried to be polite.

"We don't allow Danielle to listen to MTV music," another spit out.

"It's just 'N Sync," I said weakly. Thank God he didn't load his brother's Snoop Doggy Dogg songs. Cameron bobbed his head to his favorite line, "Baby that's no lie . . ."

"Maybe you should turn it off," someone offered. "Baby bye bye bye . . ."

When little Anibel started clapping her hands, I closed my eyes and prayed. Cross-contamination. This could be real trouble. Angelic-looking Michael dropped his book and jiggled. Danielle—

Miss Appropriate—let out a boisterous whoop. This time, I knew, the moms would take action. I removed the batteries from the CD player and begged my baby to look remorseful.

Cameron and I—dangerously close to expulsion since the Remote Control Incident, in which he quickly mastered the parental code at Cody's house and forced the other babies to watch *The Simpsons*—needed to find a group more in sync with our lifestyle.

"Too much television," I heard someone say.

Well, maybe. But I don't blame the media for my toddler's taste in music or popular culture. I lay the blame squarely where it belongs: on his siblings. They are—all three of them—teenagers of the worst stripe: honor students. Dirty laundry hiders. Pathetically bad liars. Lovers of bathroom jokes. Secret *South Park* watchers. Athletes and student council members and computer hogs.

His sister—a shoe-in for the title of Last Baby in This Family just thirteen short years ago—turns into Xena the Crazy Warrior Girl at the first sign of a debate. She passionately believes that eighth-graders are excellent drivers and that the next pope should be a woman. She taught my sweet, innocent baby to scream "Why?" and "So what?" I see law school in her future.

Cameron's fourteen-year-old brother—original owner of the notorious 'N Sync CD—fills his vocabulary with Dragonball Z names and his room with plastic creatures that have interchangeable heads. He taught Cameron that water in a sippy cup is bad, but water in a two-dollar sports bottle is good. Apple juice is bad, but Sprite is good. Graham crackers are bad, but Twinkies are good . . .

With my sixteen-year-old, Cameron discovered the deep end of the swimming pool and how high a basketball rim really is. He learned not to eat raw potatoes and how to spit for distance—useful skills for the millennium, I'm sure.

With these mini-adults around, I can't always filter out the sights and sounds of popular culture. Does Cameron need to know the difference between Nike and Fila? No. But he does need to stroll the mall on his big brother's shoulders, pretending to be king of the world. He could live without Nintendo games and virtual racetracks; but he shouldn't miss those whispery, giggly moments in his sister's lap, her hands guiding his.

As the playgroup moms gathered up their toddlers and their toys, I knew it was our last playdate; their lives and ours were hopelessly out of sync. Their babies lived a controlled and purified existence; my baby had an army ready to sneak him candy or dunk him in the fish tank. Waving bye-bye to everyone reminded Cameron of his 'N Sync song, and he ran back to the CD player. I took his hand and pulled him away.

"Mommy is older than the other mommies," I told him, using my serious, stay-on-the-sidewalk voice. "Mommy needs some quiet time. Tomorrow, Mommy's going to find some moms her own age to play with."

He smiled, a little too quickly, and scampered off to his toys. A few moments later, I heard a deep laugh. I think that kid knows where the batteries are.

KAY BOLDEN

The great thing about fads is that they fade away.
DEBRA J. SAUNDERS

THE HIGHLIGHT OF MY DAY

*E*very few months, I have to face another parenting milestone whether I'm ready or not. The last one started with my ten-year-old son announcing that he wanted to get his hair highlighted. *Fine*, I thought, *this is just a fleeting desire and I'll pretend I didn't hear.*

Unfortunately, I misjudged his passion on the subject. He kept bringing it up, first on an irregular basis, then each night before bed, and finally every hour on the hour until I had to make a definitive statement. "I don't know about this, talk to your father." Dad wasn't home at the time, and I knew I'd get to him before my son did. Luckily, my husband and I shared the opinion that while harmless, highlighting was probably something our son would lose interest in, so we'd try the stall approach.

The issue, however, stalled in my overactive imagination. Okay, I said to myself, it's only hair. It'll grow out. But he's only a kid, I argued back, and kids aren't supposed to fool with Mother Nature unless they're being toilet-trained.

I called on my inner therapist for advice. She told me I had qualms about this because of an experience four years ago when I used a hair color rinse in a fashionable shade of reddish-brown. It was supposed to last through six to eight shampoos. I made the mistake of not buying bath towels to match the hair color. And during my morning wakeup shower, the color of the water running into the drain made it appear as though I was bleeding from every pore. My legs and feet could have been used as stand-ins for a re-enactment of the famous murder scene in *Psycho*. So, the inner therapist concluded, maybe my highlighting fears weren't realistic.

I'll credit my son for being tenacious if nothing else, because he continued his campaign for highlighting. After a brief parental discussion, we proceeded into the research phase. I got out the Yellow Pages and asked him to tell me specifically what he wanted. He said that only the top front section should be highlighted. He even offered to save up his allowance to pay for it, if necessary. All three salons quoted me twenty-five dollars for the service.

Twenty-five dollars for six square inches of hair, at most, to be bleached? It couldn't take more than an ounce of generic Clorox, which, at $1.49 a gallon, amounts to . . . not very much. We suggested our son ask his friends where they'd had it done, hoping he would either find a cheaper place or drop the subject entirely.

A few nights later, I planned to meet a girlfriend for dinner, so it was going to be boys' night at home. My husband said he'd take our son to the drugstore and check into highlighting kits. I still wasn't comfortable with the idea, but at this point it was two against one. Besides, no matter how badly the job was botched, his hair would grow out soon enough, and undoing it was far less painful and expensive than removing a tattoo, right? As I drove to the restaurant, I conjured up images of hair the color of lemon drop candy or earwax: both sticky but not pretty pictures.

When I arrived back home, it was all over: the box of L'Oreal Chunking, the rinsed-off plastic highlighting bonnet, and the towel. My son sat at the kitchen table, spooning mushy microwaved ice cream into his mouth. The front of his hair—combed up in spiky peaks—was a pleasant shade of golden yellow, providing a nice contrast with his brown hair and tanned skin. I sat down next to him and looked straight at the top of his head. "What do you think?"

"It's perfect!" he replied.

"You look like you're ready to join the Backyard Boys."

"BackSTREET, Mom. And I don't listen to them anymore."

I reached toward him for a prickly feel. "Well, I think your hair is perfect too."

He ducked away. "Stop! You'll mess it up." I didn't dare ask how he would keep his hairstyle looking good while he slept.

My son went to bed happy that night. And I went to bed knowing that another parenting milestone had been hurled at me and caught. Maybe not gracefully, but caught nonetheless. I wondered, though, how well I'd do the next time. What if he asks for a body piercing?

My imagination on overdrive, I climbed out of bed and tiptoed into his room. The hallway light illuminated his blond spikes. I gazed at my sleeping punk-angel and smiled, feeling certain that accepting his new look had been the right decision. My imagination countered with "Can you handle a nose ring or a pierced eyebrow?" I made a mental note to hide the ice cubes and safety pins before the next dinner out with my girlfriend. Boys may be boys, but there are times when mother knows best.

MARILYN D. DAVIS

THEY'RE BACK!

*I*t's not that I'm ungenerous or set in my ways. It's just that for almost as long as I can remember, summers were spent lazy, carefree, and child-free. The children played tennis, swam, and wrote letters to a mother whose sole responsibility was to send occasional care packages and come to see them on Visiting Day.

Years of sleep-away summer programs provided me with ample fodder to deal subsequently with the out-of-state college years. So I am now totally ill-equipped to deal with two steady live-ins: one in between semesters, the other in between leases.

Once they left home, I was amazed at how easy it was to get used to driving a car with the seat set in a position where my foot could always reach the gas pedal. No more. The six-footer is back in town.

I had almost taken for granted the fact that turning my radio on would bring me Mozart or Bach. No more. My daughter prefers the Rolling Stones.

Gifted in spatial relations, both boarders still find it impossible to park using only one side of the garage. When I pull up in my husband's car, laden with packages from the supermarket, I can count on finding my car smack in the middle of the garage, straddling two spaces and making entry impossible.

The law of averages say that this generally happens when neither child is in the house to respond to the frantic beep of the horn. Same law also says that it is pouring outside.

Call me compulsive, but I believe it is my given right to pull open the desk and find the phone directory exactly where it is supposed to be. Same for the aspirin in the medicine cabinet.

Call me grouchy, but I've become accustomed to hearing my messages straight from the answering machine and not third-hand from my son several days after he was told by my daughter to make sure and tell me. Call me spoiled, but it's annoying to have to put on reading glasses to sort the jockey shorts by sizes instead of tossing them all into my husband's drawer.

My daughter cannot understand why I don't share her views that pooling wardrobes is a sensible idea. Here's how it goes: I get to borrow one of her micromini skirts, a stenciled zebra vest, and a fringed disco bag in exchange for my Ralph Lauren slacks, silk charmeuse blouse, and leather jacket. Stockings are up for grabs and costume jewelry doesn't count. Returns are handed over the banister in the hall, neutral territory.

My son is puzzled to find out that we've called all his friends' parents, the local taxi service, and the nearest police precinct when he arrives home at the crack of dawn. Certainly his resident counselor at school, a second-semester sophomore, would know better than to have embarrassed him like that.

Using Socratic logic and looking at us as if we had just arrived from another planet, he will ask, "Would you have wanted me to awaken you at 1:00 A.M. to tell you I'd be home at four?"

But just when I feel that I could give a seminar on "Happiness and the Empty Nest Syndrome," strange things begin to happen. My son will sympathetically respond to an excruciating muscle spasm, massaging away the pain in my neck with those wonderful fingers strengthened by years of guitar. Or wolfing down one of his favorites—homemade lasagna—he will pick me up three feet in the air for one of his famous flying hugs.

And my daughter? She will bring home flowers and explain patiently and lovingly why I should use forest-green eyeliner or let my hair grow an inch longer. And sometimes she will pour out her heart to me and actually seek the advice of someone—well, someone old enough to be her mother.

JUDITH SLOAN

A CHRISTMAS SURPRISE

Christmas was coming in a few weeks and I was being a real Scrooge. Our car decided to break down on the trip to bring my youngest daughter, Beth, home from college some fifty miles away. The temperature gauge went all the way up to hot and stayed there. Luckily for me, I found a garage nearby, but had to leave the car there overnight so they could find the problem. I called my son David to come and rescue me, and we continued to get Beth.

The weather was snowy and the ride home was long due to the bad road conditions. When we did get home we received a call from our other daughter, Andrea, telling us how she skidded into the car in front of her.

Fortunately, she was not hurt.

Tomorrow will be a better day, I thought as I tried to fall asleep.

The next day, my husband, Joe, and I juggled the car situation around so that everyone had a ride to work and back.

I was still trying to get into the Christmas spirit but it wasn't working. My job as a floral designer was draining, especially at this time of year.

"I decorate everyone else's house for the holidays," I mused, "but I'm too tired to decorate my own." I was also trying to set money aside for my son David's upcoming wedding in May. This was no time for my car to be sick. Not with Christmas shopping to do!

That night after work, I started to load the dishwasher. My glance fell on the Christmas ornaments I had set out for the children to decorate the tree with. They were still in the boxes, untouched. I began to cry out of sheer frustration. David came into the kitchen and asked me what was wrong.

"Everything is wrong," I said. "I put up the tree myself and put the lights on, and you children can't even find the time to decorate it. And now I have to pay for car repairs. This will be a fine Christmas!" I railed sarcastically. "Bah humbug!"

"Well, Dad called and the car is ready. How about I take you to get it, Mom?"

On the way to the garage, David made small talk. In the car, he played a few carols on his CD player. I sat in the front seat with tears silently spilling down my cheeks, thinking of our financial setback and wondering how I was going to afford the gifts on the children's lists. When I paid the mechanic, I angrily mentioned that my children wouldn't be having much of a Christmas now. Even though I realized the situation was not his fault, I tried to make him feel as bad as I did.

Driving home I prayed that whatever was wrong with the car was fixed now. I talked to the Lord and told Him that I really needed to have a sense of His presence.

"This time of year is too holy to go around feeling like a mean old Grinch. I need the Christmas Spirit and I need it soon! Time is running out!"

Arriving home, the first thing I noticed as I walked up to the house was an ornament hanging in the window. It was the soldier made out of toilet tissue tubes and a paper towel tube that David made in kindergarten many years ago. *What's that doing there?* I thought. Entering the living room I immediately noticed that the tree was almost decorated. Beth had put the ornaments on while we were getting the car. I smiled, thanked her, and decided to bring out the Christmas cards to address.

"Let's listen to some Christmas carols, Mom," Beth said.

She thought that would help lift my mood a bit. I went to the closet and rummaged around until I found the box of Christmas music. Setting the box of tapes on the table, Beth came over to help select some songs.

"Hey, what are these?" she asked.

"Oh, they're family tapes," I said, "but I don't remember what's on them. Let's play them and listen."

For the next two hours we listened to several tapes I had made nearly eighteen years ago when the kids were small. We could not afford a video camera so I recorded tapes, usually at the Christmas season. At first it was hard to tell who was who but we figured it out by the dates written on the cassettes.

We laughed so hard we cried while listening to their joyful, boisterous singing. Beth was actually lying on the floor from laughing so hard. In my mind, I could see my children's faces as they were then.

Brian, my oldest boy, who always seemed as if he had stars in his eyes, singing "Rudolph the Red-Nosed Reindeer" and "Frosty the Snowman."

And I could see David, my second son, who was never at a loss for words, chiming in.

I imagined Andrea, my oldest daughter, helping her mommy with the cookies.

Beth, my youngest, who never wanted to be left out of whatever her older siblings were up to, helping with the dishes.

I had asked God for a sense of His presence but He must have thought I said, "presents." Each time a new segment of the tape was played it was as if I were unwrapping present after present. I remembered how I had played the piano and each child took turns singing into the tape recorder. I heard my grandmother's voice again and the voices of my husband's grandparents, now gone. I listened to my babies giggle and belly laugh and sing at the top of their lungs.

"We have to make copies of these, Mom," said Beth. "It's so neat to hear what I sounded like when I was small."

The car problems were forgotten. I went to bed smiling that

night and thanking God for such a wonderful Christmas surprise. Hearing the tapes again made me realize what is important in life. Certainly not the car or money. What's important is my family!

I had experienced an attitude adjustment within a few hours all because of some long-forgotten cassette tapes that contained priceless memories. I was now ready to sing as my children did long ago, "Joy to the world, the Lord has come." He had come to me that night in the happy sounds of Christmas past and through the voices of my children and loved ones. My Christmas Spirit had finally arrived!

KRISTINE ZIEMNIK

An easy-going husband is the one indispensable comfort of life.
OUIDA

MEN AND THEIR FRUIT

A pattern is emerging as I regard the habits of men. Granted, I don't peek in windows and I've not done a scientific study, but I believe that most men seem to have an uneasy relationship with fruit. This report comes after a thorough study of the men in this family . . . and another guy.

Wouldn't you think that picking up a piece of fruit and chowing down on it would be a likely thing for a man to do when roaming the kitchen, looking for something good?

Often I will ask, want some cherries? They're really good.

No thanks.

How about a peach? They're perfect.

Nope. Maybe on my cereal in the morning. Thanks, though.

Orange?

Nah.

Clementine? Bosc pear? Fresh fig?

Leave me alone. Wait. Got any Fig Newtons?

Men should be dipping into the centerpiece, the bowl on the counter, the drawer in the fridge. But they don't. Men will stand in front of the fridge looking doleful for long minutes. Should they make a sandwich? Is there any pizza left over? Maybe just reach in and grab a slice of ham. Then reach in again and grab a slice of cheese. Maybe just try to sneak a slug of juice from the bottle without getting caught. Are they hungry? Trying to cool off? Hoping someone will bound in from another room and say, "Why, you poor thing. Let me make you an omelet with onions and peppers and cheese and mushrooms. I could whip up a hollandaise to go over it." That never happens.

Meanwhile, the fruit is giving up and sagging in the bowl and in the drawer, getting spotty, bruised, and soft. Neglected. At which point, the female person, who is eating some fruit but not all the fruit, takes the rest and makes a Smoothie out of it, or Banana Apple Betty, or Rotten Fruit Kuchen (which always drips in the oven and makes a very bad mess).

Here's the mystery. Men don't hate fruit. But they will only eat it under certain circumstances. Despite the cave pictures drawn of men hunkered on their haunches gnawing on other haunches . . . when snacking, modern men like small things. Small things that won't surprise them with seeds or cores or pits or internal critters hiding deep in the pulp.

A friend of mine who always has cut-up fruit in a bowl in her refrigerator mentioned one time that she takes the seeds out of the watermelon before she adds it to the bowl.

Why? Why would she bother?

Michael doesn't like the seeds.

What? (I believe I screamed.)

She is a very busy woman with a demanding career. She takes guff from no one. She seeds the watermelon? Because her husband won't work around a seed? How could this be?

When we visit them, I notice my non-fruit-eating husband always happily has a bowl of fruit.

Finally I said, "All this fruit is going to waste. Why will you eat fruit at Arlene's house?"

"Oh, she cuts it up all so nicely. I'd eat fruit all the time, if you did that."

Hmmm, if I core and cut the cantaloupe, peel the kiwi, buy

seedless grapes, cut up the tangelos into chunks, and toss them all together in a bowl, I'll have a customer? Well, OK. But I'm not seeding any watermelon.

Mystery solved. It was seed anxiety.

I'm glad that my husband will now eat fresh fruit. Still, you can't get me to seed the watermelon. I've got limits. I've got dignity.

Arlene was delighted to know that she'd caused a fuss in my house. She seemed quite happy to be blamed for spoiling my perfectly good husband.

I got her back, though, last time we were there. Boldly, I took charge of making the fruit bowl for the evening. I asked for a melon baller.

Silence.

Arlene stopped, thought, and remembered where the tool was, still in its package from her wedding shower twenty years ago.

As I was serving, I insisted to Michael that it was critical to use a melon baller because fruit, you see, is soft and lush. It isn't meant to be knifed into chunks with harsh edges. It should be rounded and sensual, and . . . I made it up as I went along.

Arlene's husband demands rounded fruit now or he won't eat it. Not without a fond reminder of how much better melons are when served in the proper small shape, the way Beverly does it.

And, back at home, I now buy seedless watermelon.

BEVERLY C. LUCEY

EIGHT GOING ON EIGHTEEN

like most parents I fantasize about having a loving, nurturing relationship with my child.

So during the first seven years of my daughter's life, I tried to follow all of the recommendations from the top childhood experts. I spent quality time with her at interesting places, used positive reinforcement and praise to build high self-esteem, and created a strong family bond by fostering a sense of love and togetherness. I also taught her how to play a mean game of jacks.

I imagined us, when she got older, being like a family on the cover of a magazine or on a television sitcom.

Then she turned eight.

I've always thought of it as a nice, nonthreatening age, except I can't get used to the fact that one moment my daughter is hosting a tea party with her dolls, and the next, covering most of her body parts with temporary tattoos.

I was caught completely off guard until a close friend explained to me that "eight" isn't really an age at all; it's more of a holding pattern between childhood and adolescence.

At first I tried to ignore the early signs—like her refusal to hold my hand when we crossed the street or her request that I stop standing up in the bleachers and yelling things like "Bubble Gum and Tootie Fruity We Got the Power to Whoop Your Bootie! Yee Haw!" during her soccer games.

I finally got the message when she began interrogating me on our way to her new classroom for third-grade orientation.

"Mom, I don't want to hurt your feelings," she said, "but you aren't going to wear your long denim skirt again, are you?"

"Yes, in fact, I am. Why?"

"Oh, no reason," she said. "But you're not going to wear the matching floppy hat with the big silk flowers, too. Right?"

"Well, I was considering . . ."

"And please don't go and ask all those questions about things like grades and stuff, OK?"

"Well, I—"

"You know," she said, matter-of-factly, "my desk is real small and it would be hard for you to sit in wearing a long skirt and all. But there are a lot of bigger chairs in the back of the room." She smiled brightly.

The more she talked, the more I grew suspicious that a teenager had somehow invaded the eight-year-old body of my little girl.

After all, how could this be coming from the same person who, since she was three, thought I was the prettiest, coolest, and smartest person in the world?

This couldn't possibly be the same girl who once insisted on wearing her fairy princess costume, accessorized with a pair of furry pink plastic high heels and a purple feather boa, everywhere she went for six months.

Or the very child who had, just the other day, looked up at me with both arms outstretched and shouted, "Turn me around and spin me, Mom!"

I finally arrived at her classroom: a broken, silent, hatless woman wearing a pair of plain jeans. I obediently sat in one of the "big chairs" in the back of the room along with the other hatless parents and tried to look as if I didn't actually know anyone in the third grade—as if I had just wandered in off the street to take a little rest.

As the school year progressed, I wasn't sure how I felt about the two versions of my daughter, especially since I could never be quite sure which one I was dealing with.

Like the time I sat down in the recliner and was stabbed by a bottle of contraband fire-engine-red nail polish. I waited until my daughter wasn't looking, then carefully slipped it into the trash. Two days later I found it in the bathroom behind the soap dispenser. So I hid it in my medicine cabinet. She put it on her dresser. I stuffed it into the big garbage can in the garage and gloated over my parental victory. Then she fished it out and painted it on her toenails.

Shortly after that, she came home from school, put one hand on her hip, and announced that if anyone should need her, she would be upstairs in her "apartment" doing her homework.

At first I didn't know what to make of it. Then I decided to go along with it since referring to her bedroom as her apartment would make the rest of the house mine, at least in theory, without having to wait ten more years.

I fantasized about sitting all alone in my spotless living room, wearing my long denim skirt and floppy hat, belting out songs like "Tie a Yellow Ribbon 'Round the Old Oak Tree" with all of the windows open. And standing up to shout soccer cheers any time I felt like it. Or being able to watch all of the talk shows and listen to seventies music on the stereo. Maybe even dance!

But as she closed the door behind her, I wasn't sure if I was ready for all that freedom yet. Especially since, deep down, I can hardly believe the baby I used to crochet sweaters for wants to wear designer jeans and trendy shoes. I feel sad thinking that upstairs, in her eighty-five-square-foot, pastel-pink apartment, my daughter is lost somewhere between fairy tales and training bras.

But occasionally my little girl returns.

Like the other day. After three hours of not speaking to me because I wouldn't let her wear lipstick to school, she looked at me with big, innocent eyes and asked me to tell her again what color gown the tooth fairy wore—and what exactly she did with all of those teeth. And if I were "absolutely sure" that she would be able to find our house, much less the tooth hidden underneath her pillow.

I smiled and reassured her, like so many times before, that the tooth fairy couldn't possibly miss our house since it was the only one on the block with Christmas lights on it in July. I told her, once again, that the tooth fairy wears a translucent blue gown with silver glitter sparkles and a magic golden crown. And definitely no lipstick. And I explained that she flits about collecting teeth strictly as a hobby. Her real job is being the chief executive of a lucrative denture company, which she earned by doing her math homework without her mother telling her and going to a good four-year college. But I can tell that she doesn't really believe me.

In fact, I almost expect her to blurt out "No way!" then lunge for my lipstick and announce that she has, at last, found a bigger apartment in a trendier neighborhood and will be moving out on her own first thing tomorrow morning.

But instead she stretches her arms up to me, and shouts, "Turn me around and spin me, Mom!"

I smile, then put my arms around her and hold her tight as we spin.

DEBBIE FARMER

Parenthood: that state of being better chaperoned
than you were before marriage.
MARCELENE COX

ROMANCE INTERRUPTED

The other day I was standing in line at Wal-Mart when I happened to notice a poster advertising a romantic getaway to Maui. A laughing blond woman was embracing her handsome partner in the bright Hawaiian sunshine. The caption read, "The best thing about our vacation? Licking the salt off my husband's margarita."

My first thought was they must not have kids. My second thought was I can't remember the last time Andrew and I were romantic, much less away somewhere alone. Then I realized that my husband and I desperately need a little privacy. You see, we have two young daughters who have been barging into our hearts and, unfortunately, our bedroom ever since they were born.

It's now St. Valentine's Day and, due to a tight budget and a lack of available baby-sitters, Andrew and I have decided to put the kids to bed and indulge in a late-night, romantic steak dinner in the privacy of our own dining room. Sounds like a good plan, right? We make the dinner, light some candles, and whisper our love for each other across the table, careful not to wake the children with loud talk or clinking glasses. For dessert we enjoy raspberries and cream, then I lead my husband into the family room, sit him on the couch, and tell him to wait while I slip into some-thing more comfortable.

I re-enter the room, turn on some barely audible music to set the mood, and begin to dance for him. Needless to say, Andrew is extremely happy that this woman who is a full-time mommy, this woman who repeatedly crawls into bed beside him with barely enough energy to offer a kiss goodnight, has been transformed into a sex goddess right before his eyes. And then we hear a tiny knock on the closed hallway door.

"Daddy? Daddy?" a little voice whispers. We freeze. "Daddy!" Elena begins to wail. I throw the afghan from the couch around my shoulders as Andrew gets up to open the door, clearly disap-pointed. "What is it, honey?" he asks our two-year-old impa-tiently. "Juice, juice," she answers. The passion has vanished like a wisp of smoke, but once she is tucked safely back in her bed, we try to rekindle it.

I slowly resume my dance, the smile creeps back onto my husband's face, and we exchange a few passionate kisses. The hall-way doorknob squeaks and begins to turn. We jump. I hurriedly don the couch afghan once again as our four-year-old walks into the room, rubbing her eyes in the light. "Mommy? Mommy, I had a bad dream," she says. "It's okay, go back to bed," I say a little too quickly. "No, I'm scared," she says. The passion has been doused. The moment is gone.

Now, you might think that the solution to our problem is sim-ple. Just lock our bedroom door and hide inside. But you don't un-derstand.

Yesterday I arrived home from one of my excursions to find a perfectly round, gaping hole in my bedroom door where a door-knob used to be! It seems Andrew had found himself locked in while I was gone and no amount of wiggling or jiggling of the temperamental doorknob had released him from his sudden prison. Our daughters, on the other side of the door, could do nothing but offer words of encouragement while my poor husband worked to remove the doorknob and pry the doorjamb from the lock.

So now we have no bedroom doorknob and no chance for privacy. We really need to get away. Our anniversary is coming up this month and we have no plans. Somehow, we're going to have to find a reliable baby-sitter so we can sneak away to a love nest somewhere. Otherwise, I'm afraid, Andrew and I will be celebrating our sixth year of wedded bliss snuggled up in our king-size bed . . . separated only by the two little girls sleeping between us.

BETH M. SKARUPA

GOING UP AGAINST MRS. SUTTON

I remember, *while growing up, having a neighbor lady, who constantly* complained to her children when they didn't straighten their rooms, study hard, or clear the supper table. Mrs. Sutton would get extremely frustrated and start "ranting" at all of them.

Granted—she had *four.*

Four children. I suppose that would give anybody certain inalienable rant-rights. After all, two or three are a handful, yes?

But it was one specific "ranting" that made me happily climb the fence and return home, each suppertime: Looking from one child to another, she would yell, "Four kids is four too many!"

Now, first of all, I think the proper grammar would actually be, "Four kids *are* four too many"—considering that "kids" is a plural word.

Second, I've wondered ever since: ". . . Did she really mean it?"

Probably not. She likely was, in effect, just a woman on the edge who needed to "vent."

But hearing her say it to her own children, I did, and still do, have a problem with. After all, if *I've* remembered it this long—then they surely have, too.

When I started having children, I determined never to say such things to mine as Mrs. Sutton said to hers, even in the unlikely event that I ended up with four. I knew (as she should have, also) that it would only make each child wonder, "If she didn't want us all, was it *me* she'd rather have skipped?"

So it was that when we recently decided to add a fourth child to our family, Mrs. Sutton immediately came to mind.

I wonder, now, what she would say if she were here. You see, I'm fairly certain we're "adding on" in a way she could never "conceive of." We're adopting.

I love my children. They're boisterous, wacky, and often quite loud. But they've intertwined just enough seeds of brilliance to warm me to the idea of shelling out for one more set of eyeglasses, braces, and childhood immunizations.

I suppose I sensed some need to add to the omnipresent mayhem. Adoption, I felt, would grant me the greatest chance to expand emotionally, without further expanding physically.

After all, we might have stopped at three offspring if we anticipated quiet bathroom time any year soon. Or if the floors had long since ceased rattling above our heads in any given room.

As for any personal, reflective meditation, *that's* been a misnomer for over a decade.

I have a teen driver who's beginning to steer with one hand. A middle-schooler who'd trade two GPA points for a date with a Backstreet Boy. And an eight-year-old whose middle name is "Bored."

Perhaps if I were used to picking up the phone without hearing, "I'm *on* here . . . !" I'd not have pursued this.

Or, if a background argument never interrupted my calling the pediatrician or plumber, I might have thought, *Golly. It's functionally quiet today. Should I really add another child and rock the boat?*

But didn't I, when the parting school bus left behind a deafening silence the other day, detect a far-off, ocean-logged cry that sounded vaguely like "Mom"?

It could have been the toddler across the street. He greets me voraciously whenever I'm outside.

But unlike his voice, this one echoed hollowly. It sounded almost like a bottled plea, calling for me to uncork and free it—before it sinks and drowns woefully offshore.

I keep wondering: Once the tide carries it in, will I really have the gumption to rock that boat (or cradle) again?

Or, will my "rusty" fingers cramp and freeze, when I grasp it anew for that first nurturing push?

I'm afraid Mrs. Sutton would never understand this. I can just hear her saying, "Three kids are *enough*. . . . Why in the world are you adopting?"

There's nothing, however, that she could say that I haven't asked myself, a hundred times or more.

What *she* would never grasp is that the hand that rocks the cradle also completes the mountainous paperwork, writes the agency checks, greets the investigating social worker, and then trembles when the phone rings after months and months of waiting.

Aw—Mrs. Sutton be darned. Let's rock.

CINDY KAUFFMAN

M&M MEDICINE

*For first-time moms like me, different stages of a child's develop-*ment can prove simultaneously frustrating and amusing. Take potty training. As soon as a child is fully trained something happens to catapult the training cycle back to Phase I.

Such was the case when my son Josiah was three. Without warning one day he began wetting himself at school, and at home. Although fully trained, he was oblivious to the problem, making me think it was an "involuntary" reaction caused perhaps by a bladder infection.

After three days of this, my concern deepened when Josiah wet himself while I was drying him following his nightly bath. As tears flooded his eyes, my son whimpered, "Mommy, I didn't feel anything."

That did it. Now I was frightened. So I called his physician, explained the problem, and scheduled a visit for early the next morning. I couldn't wait to see Dr. B., a trim, gray-haired "old-school" pediatrician who loves children and has the knack of making even the most troubled parent relax.

Upon examining my son, Dr. B. asked several questions that, to me, were unrelated to my son's current "condition." So, instead of answering him directly, I skirted around his questions in an attempt to get him to "hear" my concern. Finally, amused at my noncommittal answers, he turned to Josiah and asked, "So buddy, do you like M&Ms?" With a gleam in his eye, my son began bouncing and said, "I love M&Ms, but not with peanuts."

Turning to his assistant he ordered a urine analysis to check for possible infection, even though he admitted that was mostly likely not Josiah's problem. The negative results proved him correct.

Turning to me, Dr. B. instructed, "Mom, give him two M&Ms for every hour he is dry. I think you'll be surprised at the result." Winking at me, he began gathering up Josiah's chart as he prepared to leave the examination room.

Before I could gather my thoughts, a jubilant Josiah began whirling around the room singing "I'm going to have some M&Ms, I'm going to have some M&Ms!"

Mystified, his doctor turned to me for explanation. Ruefully I explained that I had recently reduced Josiah's "treats" to only one small piece of chocolate a week. Hearing this, Dr. B. chuckled and said, "I know you'll be happy with the results."

Amazingly, the M&M prescription worked. From the very first day of his treatment with the M&M medicine (as I dubbed it), my son's wetting problem disappeared. By day four, Josiah said, "Mommy, this M&M medicine really works."

LISA A. CRAYTON

IX
ALL THINGS DIVINE

The veil between us and the divine is more permeable than we imagine.

SUE PATTON THOELE

Our children are our future; they just don't know it yet.
AUTHOR UNKNOWN

SOWING SEEDS

For as long as I could remember, I had always wanted to teach little children. I was the oldest child in our neighborhood, growing up in a small Illinois town. I loved to gather the other children to play school. Of course, I was always the teacher. My own teachers in elementary school had a big influence on me. They were Franciscan Sisters and I wanted to be just like them.

I kept that dream alive through high school. Consequently, going off to college also meant going to the convent. The Sisters I joined were also the college professors who prepared me to be a teacher.

Education was the primary ministry of my community. I graduated from college eager to begin my work with children. I had extensive student teaching experience with several age groups, although my preference was for the younger children.

It wasn't the custom, in the 1960s, for Sisters to be given any voice in the matter of their teaching assignments. My community staffed a certain number of schools and we filled openings as needs arose. Our assignments were announced to us, and in the spirit of our vow of obedience, we simply went wherever we were directed to go. With great excitement and anticipation, my class-

mates and I awaited our first assignments after college graduation.

There was hesitation and some fear too. We wouldn't be together anymore: twenty-four of us who had gone through college
and religious formation together for five years. We would be
spread out over a number of states, living in houses with Sisters
we didn't know yet, and facing our first year in a classroom.

I will never forget the day that first assignment was given to me.
I was stunned, frightened, and all my eager readiness went plung-
ing into gloom. Because of an opening in our girls' academy and
because of my college major, I was assigned to teach math in high
school! I hadn't done any student teaching there, I hadn't wanted
to work with older students, and to add humiliation to misery, I
realized that I was failing my first test in obedience. How could I
spend a lifetime with my vows if I was already rebelling the first
time I was asked to do something?

It was a miserable summer from June to August, graduation
until the start of the school year. I tried to convince my superiors
that I wasn't right for the job, but they wouldn't change my assignment. I tried to prayerfully prepare myself for the task, but
my heart wasn't in it. I prepared my classroom before the opening
days of school, posting this quotation on the bulletin board: *Life is
not a problem to be solved, but a mystery to be lived.* Part of me said
that was a clever quotation for a math room. Another part of
me wanted to embrace the mystery and move forward in trust.
Mostly, though, I was still just rebelling inside.

The first months came and went with all the difficult adjust-
ments of new living quarters, new living companions, and the trials of being a new teacher. October came, and I still hadn't made
the attitude adjustment that was so needed if my obedient "yes"
was ever going to be anything more than lip service. My heart was
not yet in what I was doing. Then I had the dream:

*I was walking out the back door and across a field away from the
school. As my pace quickened, I dug deep into my pockets and brought*

out seeds to drop on the ground. The seeds fell on all different kinds of soil. The more I scattered the seeds, the more my walking slowed down until, finally, I wasn't running away anymore. I turned around and peacefully returned to the school.

When I woke up, I remember thinking what a strange dream that was. Then I promptly forgot about it as I prepared for the school day.

At the end of that day, as I was leaving the school, I stopped by the chapel for a quick prayer. Choosing a bench in the back because I was in a hurry, I sat down and took a deep breath. I noticed a book someone had left in the bench and I picked it up, seeking a random bit of wisdom. The book fell open to a commentary on the Gospel story of the sower and the seed. The words that instantly pierced my soul said that the seed is the word of God and we are the sowers. God depends on us to sow the seed wherever we are . . . and if we run away from the task, then there will be no one to do the particular job God has given us.

I dropped the book as the dream came flooding back to my consciousness in full detail. To say that I experienced an attitude adjustment is an understatement! Tears flooded my eyes as I wondered at the mystery of that very personal touch. God had given me a message and it couldn't have been any clearer. From that day on, the seed became my very special symbol . . . and I was finally able to say yes to where I was and to what I had been called to do.

Now, looking back on many years of teaching in high school, I smile at the memories of the "sowing." A teacher doesn't always get to see the harvest, but I was fortunate, just last summer, to spend several precious hours with a former student whose life moves me to humble gratitude for having been part of her growth.

Jane was and is a seeker. She came to high school in Ohio fresh from the death of her father, a police officer. She embraced life with wonder and caring. I took her and several other students to the Appalachians during Christmas vacation one year. We spent time with a mental health nurse and midwife, who took us to some of the homes of the mountain families. The seed was planted for Jane's future as a social worker. That was in the 1970s.

Over the years we stayed in touch, mostly through Christmas letters, and a couple times with visits, though our separate journeys took us many states apart. I followed her career and marriage and the birth of her sons. Then last summer when a workshop opportunity took me to California to a place within miles of Jane's home, we renewed a contact long overdue. We met on the grounds of a retreat center and shared the stories of our lives. Jane is a social worker, counselor, personal coach, and writer. Her eyes glow with life when she talks about her family and her work. The awesome climax of our visit was the silence we shared as we, separately but together, walked the labyrinth present on the grounds.

It was such a different walk from the one in my dream so many years ago. Then I was walking away until choosing to walk back . . . and I was alone, except for a pocketful of seeds. Now, as if in a waking dream, I was walking a twisting path, moving in and out from a sacred center. And I wasn't alone. Jane, together with my memories of so many other seeds sown, accompanied me . . . and the walking was on hallowed ground.

KAREN BERRY

ABBY'S FIGHT

On February 21, 1996, our daughter, Abigail, was born. She gave out one small, helpless cry then ceased breathing on her own. She was not perfect. She was not healthy. But she was a fighter.

Abby was hooked up to life-support systems and transported from our hospital in Bakersfield, California, to the Neonatal Intensive Care Unit (NICU) at UCLA—over one hundred miles from the home that we had excitedly prepared for her during the previous thirty-five weeks. Upon her arrival at UCLA, she was diagnosed with a rare cystic kidney disease that caused her kidneys to grow so large that the weight of her abdomen interfered with her ability to eat or breathe. Ten years ago this diagnosis was a death sentence. And while the specialists at UCLA held out some hope, my Abby's prognosis was not good.

For almost ten weeks, my husband, David, and I scrubbed in and donned sterile gowns in the hopes of bringing our daughter some measure of comfort. Because Abby was on a respirator we could not hear her cry, but we could see her pain and anguish as we watched her endure hours of poking and prodding instead of the cuddles and cooing we had anticipated. It was the most heart-wrenching experience of our lives. And while we knew that it was all in her best interest, there were indeed times when I wondered if our heroic efforts were worth the pain and suffering our beautiful daughter was having to withstand. I sat, watched, and waited for a miracle.

Finally, on April 5, 1996, Good Friday, the specialists decided to remove one of her kidneys in the hope that it would give her enough relief to let her breathe on her own but still leave her with some kidney function to avoid dialysis until she was bigger and stronger. The thought of this milestone thrilled us. But we knew that the surgery came with risks, and nobody really knew if it would work.

Abby came out of surgery that Friday evening with the doctor smiling and amazed at the size of the two-pound kidney (25 percent of her body weight) that he had just removed. He was pleased with the surgical procedure, but it would be "wait and see" for the kidney function and respiratory issues. We attended Easter services at a nearby church and fervently prayed for our child. We even managed some comic relief as I noticed that the security tag had been left on the leg of my husband's new pants. He had dressed for church without ever noticing, illustrating how truly distracted we were.

We spent Easter in the NICU with friends and family bringing goodies beyond our wildest imaginations. Abby slept. Her kidney function, while seriously impaired, did stabilize. Now for the breathing . . .

The doctors told us it would be ten to fourteen days before Abby could try coming off the respirator due to the length of time she had been on the machines and her weakened state from the surgery. With that information and after calling and checking in with Abby's nurse, Monday morning we went to the local mall to get the security tag off Dave's pants and to have some coffee. As we sat chatting, David's pager went off. The number read "310 825—." The numeric message was incomplete, but it was definitely the first few numbers for the NICU. My heart sank, and I feared the worst. In our many weeks at UCLA nobody had ever paged us. The nurse knew we were coming soon, so I figured it must be serious.

David called from a pay phone and spoke to Abby's nurse, Bess. He returned to me with his eyes so wide that I almost burst into tears from all of my thoughts of what could have happened to my baby. He said, "Bess said that *nobody* paged us, but—you're not going to believe this—she's off the respirator as of two minutes ago and doing great!" A chill ran through me at that moment. I instinctively knew that we must have been paged by Abby's angel to witness the miracle for which we had prayed.

As I held my child for the first time on her "breath day," I was transformed. This experience would redefine the concept of miracle for me and comfort me on the difficult journey that was to come. By the time Abby was twenty months old, she had endured countless doctor visits, labs, more surgeries, four months of home dialysis, and eventually a transplant, receiving my left kidney.

As challenging as it has been over the last several years, Abby's been a great teacher for us. We've learned that it's not the problems handed to us in life that matter, it's how hard we put up the good fight to see them through that counts.

JULIE TEASDALE

Moments of silence are part of the music.
AUTHOR UNKNOWN

SEVEN BELLS

P eople think I'm courageous, but I don't know about that. It's true, this year I worked with—well, listened to—my intuition much more than ever before, and it affected how I did things. But the kind of knowing I experience tonight, I decide, demands too much of me. It could be downright embarrassing. So, at midnight, with my head still on the pillow, I declare, albeit to myself, that I'm not up to this. Courage? It flies out the window as I discard the message I'd just received.

A nice message. But just a message, I tell myself, as I put it on the shelf.

Well, an awesome message, my inner self answers.

True. I turn over and plump my pillow. *So very true.* I had to admit it.

But, even if it is cool and life-changing, my more pragmatic self responds, *you can still keep it to yourself.* I relax a bit. *It can be your own nugget of gold.*

Yes, I say, as I draw the blanket close around my shoulders and let sleep overtake me.

As morning comes, I blink. Ah, this day of days. *God, please lead me in my steps . . .* and instantly it comes back to me. The memory of the past night. In the tranquil time between closing my eyes and sleep, I'd been praying for Nancy's mom, who'd just passed over.

This was my courageous step, at least for me, I'd thought. Before this year, when someone died, I'd prayed for the person in mourning. The one who faced loss and needed the shelter of all of our love. But this year, I'd also started praying for the people who passed over. Praying for their souls to feel our love and care. Our celebration of them. Our thankfulness.

Funniest thing was that I hadn't known Nancy's mom. My friendship with Nancy was in its beginning stages, so I knew nothing about her family. Which was one of the reasons my fingers thumped nervously beside the phone now, instead of picking up the receiver. How could I tell Nancy about it? About the wonderful thing that had happened to me last night. What would she think of me?

I felt some consolation knowing I'd told Nancy I would pray for her mom. And I'd wanted to do more than say that. I wanted to keep my promise. This year I'd experienced a shift in my thinking and a shift in my experience. Because of tuning in to my intuition, I'd had more "Incoming" messages. It's as if I'd realized more fully there are two boxes, Incoming and Outgoing, and with that came the pleasure of receiving more Incoming thoughts. Loving ones at that.

So as I'd sent out my prayer for Nancy's mom last night, I was surprised but not completely shocked when almost immediately I felt her spirit's happy, even humorous voice meet up with my thoughts: *Hey, thanks for contacting me!*—As if she'd been waiting!

Nancy's mom didn't wait upon ceremony, but reached out, like a melody in a song that was already playing. *Please tell Nancy, "When you need me, ring a bell."*

She paused. These were simple words, but words that held such warmth. And a good dose of joy.

And tell her, "When you hear it ring, you'll remember how much I love you!"

Suddenly the night felt spacious. As I said the words over and over to myself, both to savor them and then to remember them so I could tell Nancy, I felt the ringing of the bells expand my own heart's capacity to receive.

As I searched for pen and paper in the darkness, trying not to wake my snoozing husband, one part of me said, *Sharing this is crazy!* But another part of me answered, *Sharing this is your assignment.* Since it sounded like the higher part of me, I went with it.

Lifting the receiver, I hoped for the best.

"Ah, I understand such things," Nancy answered.

Good, I said to myself, because picking up the phone was harder than receiving the incoming message!

"Thank you," Nancy said softly. "Thank you . . . boy, does that fit."

Nancy's direct, and I like that. "How's that?" I queried.

"The interesting thing is, I have another friend, Fran, who listens to angels. And her angel, John, gave me a message, too! It goes something like this, 'When you are rejoined with your mom, there will be happiness and rejoicing, in the song—and the ringing of seven bells!' "

Over the long-distance phone lines, both Nancy and I experienced chills.

Afterward, Nancy traveled east to a relative's home, where her mom had lived out her last days. Looking for something of her mother's to keep as a remembrance, she realized the home had been swept completely clean of her mother's things. No photos. Nothing. Discouraged, Nancy slumped into a dining-room chair—when something nudged her to simply look up.

"I'd forgotten my mother collected them," she explained in her next phone call.

"What was it?"

"It was a collection," she explained, the happiness once again in her voice. "A beautiful collection . . . of all kinds of bells!"

Another chill ran through us.

"Each bell was different. So many beautiful bells. In fact . . ." —her voice softened again—"there were seven."

"Ah . . ." In one moment it was as if all our worlds came together in a circle of meaning that none of us alone could have understood.

I think of this as the phone rings again today. This time it's a different person, a different set of circumstances. Jennifer's calling to move an appointment. She's completed an art project and, as a creativity coach, I'm helping her with her fear of showing her work. A studio is interested in seeing her paintings, but suddenly she's not ready and starts to stall.

As we talk, I hear more promptings from my soul again. *Don't let her move the appointment a month down the road. You know it will never happen. Speak up. Speak up!*

Pragmatically, I still don't want to be brave. To let courage direct my days. But I know bells when I hear them.

"Jen," I say . . .

And as something beautiful begins to guide my words and ways, I smile as both of us surrender to the sure, strong wisdom flowing through us, using the situation to teach us what lies beyond our habits of resistance. "Incoming," I say to myself. "Yep," I hear Jen silently respond—as not one heart, but two, are ineffably changed.

SHEILA STEPHENS

FAST FOOD FAITH

*T*oo many times I had sat that same way—shoulders slouched, head in my hands, wearing despair like an old, familiar blanket. When you don't have enough money, all you can think of is money—how much you have, how far it will go, how many days until your next paycheck. The money litany becomes a leaky faucet of thoughts, a constant dripping of worry and stress.

I sighed deeply and sat up. It's not as though I wasn't trying. As a single parent, I did everything possible to provide for my two children. However, unlike my parents and siblings, I had not graduated from college. Finding a decent paying job without a degree had been difficult. So I sold shoes in an upscale department store by day and used my experience as a beautician to do hair in my kitchen at night. The kids were used to the smell of perm solution mixing with the aroma of their SpaghettiOs.

Most of the time, on a wing and a prayer, I managed to get by on my income. Still, it was a delicate balance, and sometimes my small weekly budget disappeared way too soon.

Like right now. I sat staring at the paint-chipped walls in the upstairs apartment of the old house where we lived. I tried to lean on God and hand him my worries, but most of the time, I took them back again. I ran into God's arms when things were hard, but it was difficult to remain there.

Maybe, I thought, *I really only have a fast food faith. Maybe I expect drive-in-window solutions, with answers to my prayers all neatly wrapped—and no waiting.*

As I had done a hundred times before, I went into my kitchen and dialed Kathy's number. I was so grateful for a friend like this—someone with whom I could bare my soul.

"God knows, and He cares. Something will happen and it will all work out; I just know it," said the voice of my lifeline on the other end of the phone.

"Ah well, He'd better hurry then," I joked, absently twisting the phone cord around and around my fingers. "I only have a dollar fifty-six left in my checkbook until payday."

"He will," Kathy said with quiet conviction.

She always saw beyond my joking and knew it was my way of not crying instead.

"You're in my prayers, you know. Every night."

"I know, Kath. Thank you so much. I don't know what I'd do without you."

Somehow, some way, it would turn out.

I had a best friend who understood how difficult it was at times to hang on to my faith and trust in God. And so I let it all go again—I sent all those desperate concerns back up to Him.

"God, you know I only have a dollar fifty-six left," I told him as if we were sitting having coffee together. "I need your help; I can't do it alone anymore."

There was no bolt from heaven, no sudden rush of the Spirit filled my soul, but somehow I felt more at peace. God had turned off the constant worry that I had held on to for so long, and I was going to let things remain in His hands.

The internal peace I experienced would have been enough of an answer, even if nothing changed. But, a day later, I went down the stairs and across the street to my mailbox and pulled out a letter from another friend of mine. *Why would she write to me instead of call?* I wondered as I tore open the envelope and pulled out the note inside.

"Dear Anne," it began. "Thanks so much for doing my hair—I love it! And thanks for waiting for the money. I'm sorry it took me so long to get it to you. Patti." Inside was a check for twenty dollars that I'd forgotten she owed me. It may not seem like much, but it was exactly what I needed at that moment.

In a heartbeat, every detail around me seemed to shift to a brighter focus, the edges of the grass, the trees, everything took on a sudden sharpness, beauty, and clarity. Not a coincidental occurrence to me, but providential. I stood silent in a sacred moment. Even the sunlight dancing over the mailbox seemed alive and filled with the Divine.

Finally, reverently, I lifted my face to the skies and thanked my Father above for reminding me that having more than a fast food faith in Him fulfills me as nothing else can.

ANNE GOODRICH

THE MAN ON THE BEACH

*O*n the list of life stressors, loss of a job and death of a loved one are in the top five. I was in the top five. On the day my stepfather died, my company put into action its downsizing plan. My department was wiped off the organization chart. My job no longer existed and my beloved stepfather was beyond my reach forever.

I was struggling with a myriad of emotions in the aftermath of these devastating blows. My mother had been mentally ill since I don't know when, perhaps even before I was born. My stepfather shielded her, protected her, lived with the effects of her illness, and could never bring himself to place her anywhere.

Now he was gone, and I was left. I was now the decision maker.

Since I had no pressing job to return to after his death, I stayed with my mother, desperately trying to grasp a way to care for her on a long-term basis. After three months, my own emotional well-being was strained to its limits. My aunt, who lived three blocks away, agreed to become more involved with my mother on a day-to-day basis. With her help and with the resources of outside agencies, we embarked on a see-how-it-goes trial period to keep my mother in her familiar surroundings. I returned home to New Jersey to assess the fallout of my life.

Death and grief can wreak havoc on mental, emotional, and physical capabilities. I was in bad shape and knew it. To find solace, to clear my mind, to recharge my batteries, I went to the beach. The vastness of the sea with its continuous rhythmic motion was an old friend, so I went there in April to find relief for my suffering soul.

It was a stellar day. Clear blue sky, bright sunshine, white-capped waves, and the beach was deserted in every direction. A winter storm had washed up a large piling from some distant place. I sat down and stared far out at the horizon line.

Then, I looked to the left toward the old fishing pier off in the distance and spotted a lone figure walking. My attention remained on this figure while it closed the space between us. *This is an individual who walks with purpose,* I thought, taking in the pace, posture, and gait.

Closer and closer the figure approached until I could see it was an elderly man. He wore a green cap, work clothes, and jacket just as my stepfather had worn. My breath caught in my throat. I wanted to run. Run toward this figure, throw my arms around him, and never let go. Could it be? I frantically questioned. He looks just like Pap. Joy leaped in my heart. It vanished when the man got close enough for me to see it wasn't my stepfather. Down at the water's edge the man changed direction and headed up the beach toward me. He was approaching quickly so I hastily wiped away tears and blew my nose. When he got ten feet within me, he took off his cap and ran his hand across his brow.

"Afternoon," he said with a slight nod. "Mind if I sit a spell?"

"Not at all," I replied in a shaky voice. "Please join me, it's such a lovely day."

"Yep, that it is. Don't often find anyone here at this time of year. Particularly on what most folks call a workday. Guaranteed if the world keeps runnin' at such a pace, it's gonna be the death of young people, not old ones like me."

My throat was frozen, so I just nodded in reply.

"Mind taking your sunglasses off so I can see what you look like?" He asked. "Hate talking to people whose eyes hide behind dark glass."

I removed my sunglasses, squinted, then shielded my eyes from the bright sunlight with my hand.

"Nice blue eyes. But yep, those eyes look like they've been sheddin' lots of tears."

I turned my face back toward the sea. My insides were shaking. I wasn't trembling with fear of this man; it was just that there was something about him that reminded me so much of my stepfather.

"No need to worry, missy. Whatever troubles you will pass. Guaranteed to pass quickly, too. By next April, you'll be here again lookin' at the same sea, but your burden will have eased. You've got to trust in the Almighty. He's a-watchin'. Watchin' over you, and he's guaranteed to help with what's a-troublin' you."

My heart raced. There it was again! That stringing out of the word *guarantee,* just like my stepfather did. I faced the stranger. He kept his gaze out to sea. I studied his profile with intense scrutiny. He looked nothing like my stepfather, but still . . . there was that something.

"Missy, all that's a troublin' you is a bump in the road. A fine missy you are. I kin tell. A strong one, too. Always have been. You'll do what's right."

We sat like this in silence, staring out at the ocean for a long, long time. He stirred from his reverie first. "Well, missy, gotta be goin'. Nice sittin' here with you. Though can't say you talked much. But bein' the understanding man I am, I'm not holdin' you to much conversation. A troublin' heart doesn't want to do much talkin'." He stood. His shadow fell across me. "Missy, trust in the Almighty. He's a-helpin'. Might not be the kind of helpin' you're expectin'. But he's a-helpin'. Afternoon to you, now."

When I pulled myself together again to search the beach to the left and right of me, there wasn't a soul in sight.

Afterward, I thought a lot about the man on the beach. My path took me to many places, support groups, and books dealing with death, dying, and grief. I spoke with mothers, fathers, sons, daughters, widows, and widowers. I read the philosophies of different religions on the subject of death and found references on how it is not unusual for a grieving person to see or have a visit from the person who has passed on.

The ensuing months after April were filled with ups and downs, with many planned and unplanned trips back to Pittsburgh. As the Christmas holidays approached, my aunt and I agreed it was getting impossible for care for my mother at home. It was time to seek out alternative solutions. I braced myself for what was to come. In the stark moment of my anguish, I kept hearing the stranger's words: "You've got to trust in the Almighty. He's a-watchin'."

One year later I was back at the beach just as the stranger predicted, and the heavy burden of deciding how to best care for my mother had been lifted. I never had to make the decision I feared most: to place Mom in a care facility. She had died unexpectedly in February, one year and two weeks after my stepfather. The stranger's words reverberated within me: "He's a-helpin' . . . but not in a way you might be expectin'."

I sat there engulfed in a myriad of conflicting emotions of guilt and relief. A solitary gull stood before me. He seemed to be staring at me intently. Within, I heard a whisper, *Missy, it's as it should be.* Reminding me that there truly is a plan to our lives—and an invisible Divine team working behind the scenes to keep us all afloat as we ride the emotional waves to joy and peace.

GERALDINE (GERRY) TRICKLE

THE FINAL SAY

When I make up my mind to do something, I am like a woman on a mission. I wanted new shoes and I wanted them now. Sensible designer shoes—shoes with a thick heel and a funky flair. I decided to go shopping that evening.

I had two stores in mind located in opposite directions. I wanted to go to the one off the 605 Interstate in the Los Angeles area, but each time I thought about going that way, a horrible feeling of impending doom came over me. It was so strong that I paced the kitchen arguing with myself.

What could go wrong? I'm a careful driver. Maybe I should go south instead. No, I want to go to the store off the 605.

Then that terrible, dark feeling returned.

What could happen? The parking lot could be dimly lit. I could take my pepper spray.

I checked my purse to make sure I had it with me. Once more I decided to go ahead where I wanted to, and the feeling came back. I said to no one in particular, "I don't care, I'm going anyway." And with that I went out and got in my car.

The first thing I noticed was that my gas gauge was on empty. I was upset that I had to stop since it cut into my shopping time, but I had no choice, so I got gas and continued.

As I was speeding up to enter the freeway, the guy ahead of me stopped dead in his tracks. I swerved quickly to the left lane and missed him by inches. Luckily, no one else was there.

That must have been what the bad feeling was about. Now everything will be fine.

I knew that I'd feel terrible if anything happened to my little black car. It was my first brand-new car. I named her "Black Beauty," and she didn't have a scratch on her. I intended to keep it that way.

As I drove on, the feeling of doom returned stronger than ever. The trip to the store takes twenty minutes. When I pulled over onto the off-ramp near the shoe store, a car cut me off, causing me to hit the brakes hard. *Whew, that was a close call. That must have been it.*

"Third time's a charm," I said aloud. How prophetically ironic that statement would prove to be.

About forty minutes later, with my new clunky shoes in hand, I left the store. I intentionally stayed close to a group of people as I exited the mall and walked to my car.

Using my cell phone, I decided to call my daughter in San Diego on the drive home. We don't get to see each other on a regular basis because we live one hundred miles apart. I didn't tell her where I was, just that I had found some great shoes at a good price. I entered the freeway and we continued to talk.

Traffic in my lane became quite heavy after about a mile. The glare of the other headlights bothered my eyes so I adjusted my rearview mirror. In a heartbeat, the truck in front of me came to a complete stop. I slammed on the brakes and glanced in my rearview mirror and saw two headlights coming up on me at a fantastic rate of speed. The last thing my daughter heard me say was, "I don't think the guy behind me is going to st—"

I heard the squeal of brakes as the impact plunged me into my inflated airbag. Everything went black for a couple of seconds and then I was thrust upright again. My car had been shoved into the truck in front of me. Smoke filled Black Beauty and everything seemed surreal. I fumbled for the door in the dim haze and fell out of the car near the oncoming traffic.

A woman got out of the car behind me. She kept asking if I was okay. Just then, a tow truck pulled up and the driver asked if he could help. At the same time, a highway patrolman appeared on a motorcycle. He asked for our driver's licenses and proof of insurance. I hobbled back to my car to look for the papers, unaware of any danger. The patrolman finally yelled at the tow truck driver to get me out of the traffic. I was dazed and wandering around while cars swerved to avoid me.

I spotted my cell phone on the floor in the car and called my husband, Paul. He asked me where I was and arrived in record time. Upon seeing him, I crumbled against him and started to shake and cry.

Meanwhile, the policeman could see I was hurt and called for an ambulance. The paramedics arrived and checked me over. I chose to go to the hospital with Paul. I had contusions, bruises, and a cracked tooth from the impact. I had skinned my nose on the airbag, my chest had seatbelt burn, and the necklace I was wearing had made an indelible imprint on my neck.

I later learned that my daughter had become hysterical upon hearing the screech of brakes, the crunch of metal, and breaking glass. Her husband, Ed, came running in the room when he heard her yelling, "Mom, Mom!" He picked up the phone and called my name. When there was no answer, he had the operator cut the connection and called my husband. Ed told him I had been in an accident but he didn't know where. Poor Paul had been sitting by the phone waiting for my call.

While I was sitting in the emergency room waiting to be treated, my husband recounted the events of the evening. My daughter's hysteria after hearing the accident, her feeling of helplessness at not being able to talk to me, and how Ed had tried to find out my whereabouts by calling the Highway Patrol. Only then did I remember I had been talking to Jen when the accident happened. I asked Paul to call and reassure them that I was going to be all right.

I think back on that night not so long ago, and ask myself, "Are we predestined to have certain things happen to us?"

I don't think so.

I believe we are given free will and can choose to listen to God or not. There were many calls going on that night. I called my daughter, the patrolman called the paramedics, Ed and I called my husband . . . and earlier in the evening, God had called me, but I refused to heed the message.

I have never had feelings of doom so strong as I did that night. Now I realize that God can only direct our lives to the degree that we're willing to listen. Never wanting to ignore those warnings again, I've promised myself that next time—no matter what—I'll let God have the final say.

SALLIE A. RODMAN

TWO GOLD RINGS

*E*very morning, for an entire week, I dreamed that I was sitting at my grandmother's bedside. Her eyes were closed and her light hair was brushed back, revealing her delicate features. I closed my hand around hers and it felt warm and alive.

It was by chance that I found this secret place where only my grandmother and I existed. One morning as I started to rise from bed amid shouts of "Oatmeal!" and "Juice!" from my children, my husband said, "You rest. I'll give them breakfast today."

I slept for just over an hour, her hand firm and warm in mine.

I was unable to dream of her again that night. But when dawn tinged the walls of my bedroom pink and the sleepless night of twisted sheets passed, she was there.

She would be waiting for me in the small, pale room where I would cling to her hand like a frightened child. It was the room in the quiet nursing home where she was placed on hospice. The room where life left her body as softly as a golden chick sheds its shell.

Almost a year would pass before I would dream of her again.

She had been hospitalized frequently over the last few years and I was proud of the way my two daughters conducted themselves while visiting.

When my grandmother became weak, my four-year-old tenderly fed her small spoonfuls of soup while my two-year-old gave her sips from a carton of milk.

My girls spent as much time in cramped, tube-filled rooms as they did at the park. But we made do.

I like to think that they learned compassion and a sense of pride from helping me to care for my grandmother. I'm certain that they never would have loved her so deeply if I had kept them away.

I was preparing to leave for the nursing home when the call came.

"She's gone," my mother said.

And that's how, the day after her death, I began spending time with my grandmother in my dreams.

At the funeral home I removed one of my gold earrings and requested that it be sealed with my grandmother in the graceful floral urn. "You'll have half and I'll have half," I said, holding her lifeless hand. The earrings were special to me; I had worn them continuously for more than a decade.

Later that day, my mother and my aunt presented me with my grandmother's ring. I remember thinking, she is giving me a ring of gold, too. I thought our circle of giving was complete.

I felt bare without my elegant gold hoops, but I felt guilty for wanting to replace them. I bought an inexpensive pair of tiny ovals. The next day, one of them cracked in half. I returned to the store. This time I chose a sturdier pair, but lost one of them a few days later. It was all too much for me. The lost earring seemed a symbol of everything that was wrong in my life.

"Grandma," I called. "Give me a sign."

My children were asleep and my voice echoed in the quiet house.

I sat on the floor in my foyer and cried.

I'm not sure how long I wept, but when the dim foyer gradually filled with light, I rose, pulling my bare lobe in frustration. I decided to search my jewelry box. I walked to my dresser and opened the mahogany lid. On top of the neat sections of crimson velvet was a plain white box. It seemed foreign and I opened it slowly. Two perfect gold hoops sat on a square of white cotton. They were just the right size, and just expensive enough to ensure that they could be slept in, showered in, and never cause discomfort or come unhinged.

I knew this because they were identical to the pair I had worn throughout my twenties and well into my thirties.

"Thank you, Grandma," I said softly.

Although I had always been a believer in science, in plausibility, never in miracles, I decided to accept this spiritual gift with grace. Sometimes miracles can happen if we simply peer through half-closed eyes and say, "I believe."

Almost a year after my grandmother's death, my daughters and I were in a store shopping for linens.

"Grandma? Grandma!" my two-year-old daughter called.

She was pointing at the rear wall of the store, which was covered chromatically from ceiling to floor with towels. I expected to see an older woman who resembled my grandmother, but no one was there.

"Mom, she keeps calling Grandma, and she knows she's not here anymore," my four-year-old daughter said, narrowing her eyes and crossing her arms. "She knows Grandma went to heaven."

I gave her an understanding smile. "Maybe she's just remembering in her own way. And that's good." I soothed.

She gave me a knowing look. "I remember her too," she said.

"Grandma! Grandma!" they called, their voices rising like balloons.

That night, almost a year after her death, I dreamed of her again. We were alone in the department store and a mountain of the most beautiful towels I'd ever seen separated my grandmother and me. My grandmother was folding the towels with enthusiasm; there was already a tall mound forming behind her. I gave her a false smile to hide my bewilderment. I would never be able to fold all these towels and be near Grandmother again. It was hopeless.

"It's all manageable," she said in my dream, her brown eyes shining with love. "You just have to have faith."

"I do have faith, Grandma," I said, bending to pick up a towel. It was soft as velvet and shimmered with all the colors of the rainbow. I opened it wide and smiled. Emblazoned on the towel were two gold earrings.

CHRISTINE M. CALDWELL

AN ANSWER TO A PRAYER

My best friend Tama's second child, Annika, was having a difficult time. She weighed only ten pounds at seven months. The doctors called it "failure to thrive." They were running tests on the infant to determine the cause of her condition. All Tama knew was that the baby didn't want to eat. She would spend five hours a day trying to feed Annika, who would just close her mouth and avert her head. Needless to say, this mother was stressed and anxious.

Tama and her two children, three-year-old Thomas and Annika, had traveled to another city with her sister Barb due to an illness in the family. During their stay, Annika woke up at 12:30 A.M. and screamed on and off for five hours. Pacing the floor, Tama tried to comfort her wailing infant, praying for help of any kind. She finally fell into an exhausted sleep at 5:30 A.M. only to be awakened at 7:30 A.M. by Barb, who was ready to drive home.

On the car trip through the desert, Tama continued to encourage Annika to eat, to no avail. Halfway home the family stopped at a fast food restaurant with an indoor play area for Thomas. Tama took the children into the rest room where an older woman was washing her hands. The stranger offered to hold the baby for Tama while she helped Thomas. Tama was hesitant, yet the woman seemed unusually kind so she handed Annika over and went into the stall with Thomas.

The woman was saying that she loved all children, how special they are, how she wasn't partial to her own, but loved them all because they were God's children. When Tama walked out of the stall, she noticed a faraway look in the woman's eyes.

"Feed this baby buttermilk," the woman said, still holding Annika. Tama looked at her sharply; she had said nothing about the infant's condition. The woman continued, "Yes, feed her buttermilk, she'll take buttermilk, she'll grow on buttermilk, she'll thrive. The Lord is telling me this, yes, the Lord. Do you believe in the Lord?"

Taken aback, Tama said, "Well, ah, yes . . ."

The woman rushed on with her instructions, saying, "And another thing, feed her beef broth, yes, give her beef broth and also give her pureed meat. Get the finest cuts of meat, sirloin steak has the best flavor, and blend it until it's smooth as silk and feed her a little every day, she'll like it."

At this point the woman stopped, and with a considering look on her face, added, "Why, there's something wrong with this baby. There is something wrong with her digestion. It started when she was about six weeks old."

"Yes, I have been having a really hard time with her," Tama replied. "And you're right, it did start at around six weeks of age." Tama was quite flabbergasted about all this. Barb had walked into the restroom just as the woman began to speak and had witnessed it all.

The sisters looked at each other in wonder as the stranger continued to offer other things to feed Annika, such as "little bits of butter on teething toast, and carrots."

Thomas was getting restless by then, so Tama asked Barb to take him out to the play area. After they left, the woman handed Tama her child, saying, "Keep the baby's hands covered in the winter, she has poor circulation." Tama nodded in agreement, not sure what to make of everything the stranger had told her.

As Tama and the woman left the rest room, Tama looked around the seating area, curious to see whom the woman was sitting with. The restaurant was empty. As they said their farewells, Tama said, "Thank you very much. I'll take your advice because I am at my wit's end."

Tama tried everything the stranger had suggested when they got home, and over the course of a week, Annika's intake gradually went up. Within ten days, the baby was eating normally, and her mother was ecstatic! She called Barb to share the good news.

In a solemn, awed voice, Barb responded, "Oh, my God, I didn't tell you this before because it freaked me out so much. When I left you guys in the rest room and went to the restaurant next door to get burritos, that lady walked up to my car while I was sitting in the drive-through lane. Our eyes met, we smiled and nodded at each other, and she walked around the front of my car, and went past the building. I thought this was odd—no one walks into the desert. I pulled up right after her, rolling down my window to say a final thank-you, and she had completely disappeared! It was no more than a few seconds after she had stepped behind the wall, and she was nowhere to be seen. I pulled the car out and around, looking for her. There was no door she could have gone into, only desert. Tama, she must have been an angel."

Tama felt chills all over her body. To this day, she isn't sure if the woman at that roadside fast food restaurant truly was an angel, but she does know that from that day on, little Annika continued to eat well every day on the recommended foods. The pediatrician was amazed when all her metabolic tests came back normal.

Tama admits asking for divine assistance as she paced the room with her wailing infant in the wee hours of that horrible night, and angel or no, the stranger she met the next day provided an answer to her prayer. Annika is now a healthy and active eight-year-old child.

JULIE HARTMANS

Faced with unmeasurables, people steer their way by magic.
DENISE SCOTT BROWN

A BOATFUL OF ANGELS

*O*n a chilly, gray Saturday morning in Portland, Oregon, a young man stood on the Ross Island Bridge, contemplating whether his life was worth living, so depressed and downhearted that he was willing to end it all by jumping into a watery grave. He was in a lot of emotional pain. Not the kind of pain you can see like a broken bone, but pain nonetheless. His inner voice was screaming, "Don't jump!" But nobody was there to help him. He did not have an angel that he could see. Slowly he loosened his grip on the railing and leaned forward.

Out of sight, a quarter of a mile down the river, a number of us women were waiting to board a tipsy, narrow dragon boat to begin a preseason practice and prepare for the International Dragon Boat Competition.

We were not your average group of athletes. As new and returning members of the Pink Phoenix Dragon Boat team, some of us were barely acquainted. We were, however, linked by a common thread—we all had breast cancer and were holding on to life with a fierce but tentative grip. Over the years, some of our teammates had not lived, yet we were all familiar with the struggle to survive.

We paddle to demonstrate that you can have upper-body

strength and quality of life with and after cancer. In our city, we are symbols of courage and vitality. Three of us that morning were nurses with emergency room experience.

We were not all seasoned paddlers. That day, we did not even have enough women on board to legally take the boat out, but we went out anyway. Lately, we had been paddling so poorly that we had not even made it to the halfway point down the river three-quarters of the way into our practice.

So at the same time that we turned back toward shore, a young man let go of his grip on the railing and stepped off. Out in the distance, about six hundred meters upstream, we saw an unbelievable sight. Something quite large was falling from the bridge. Oh, my God, it's a man! Oh, my God.

He hit the water with a loud, hard slap. We gasped and without hesitation one of us yelled, "Let's go get him!"

Privately, as the most experienced paddler and a nurse for over twenty years, I thought we'd be too late. But our illness had given us experience with racing the clock.

"Paddles up, ladies, take it away." Swish, swish, swish in perfect harmony. For the first time in a long while, we had a compelling reason to be in sync.

When we reached the young man, he was barely conscious. We pulled him up to the gunnels and held on. Soon after, a couple of fisherman raced toward us. They had a cell phone and called 911. As they lifted the young man into their boat, we piled our coats on top of him to combat the hypothermia that was setting in. The fisherman sped with the young man to the dock where paramedics were already on the scene. He was taken to the hospital, where he was treated.

One morning, a week or two later, he came to our mooring to thank us and to tell us how much he now appreciates life. When he jumped off the bridge, he said it felt as if he was falling in slow motion. Cupped in the hand of God, some might say, to give us time to paddle over to him. As the water came up to meet him, he knew he had made a mistake, but it was too late. Until he heard the chatting of "angels" above him.

It became instantly clear to me that this was the reason Pink Phoenix had come together. Who knows, it may even be the reason we have cancer—so that we'd be in that boat, on the river that dreary, cold morning. As fate would have it, we'd all been fighting for our own lives, and the life we saved that day was his. The ladies in pink wouldn't have it any other way.

FERN CARNESS

MORE CHOCOLATE STORIES?

Do you have a true short story you want published that fits the spirit of *Chocolate for a Woman's Courage* or *Chocolate for a Woman's Soul?* I am planning future editions using a similar format, which will feature love stories, divine moments, family highlights, overcoming obstacles, following our intuition, and humorous events that allow us to laugh at ourselves. I am seeking heartwarming stories of two to four pages in length that feed your soul.

I invite you to join me in these future projects by sending your special story for consideration. If your story is selected, you will be paid one hundred dollars, be listed as a contributing author, and have a biographical paragraph about you included. For more information, or to send a story, please contact:

Kay Allenbaugh
P. O. Box 2165
Lake Oswego, Oregon 97035
kay@allenbaugh.com

www.chocolateforwomen.com

CONTRIBUTORS

MISHELE ABELL left Washington State in 1991 in search of an adventure. She began working on boats, and became a professional chef who's specialized in catering on large, private yachts, traveling the world over. She lived in Viareggio, Italy, worked part-time on yachts as a chef and as an Italian food and wine educator for Americans in Italy, and enjoys writing, reading, and studying healing arts in her free time. misheleabell@hotmail.com

BROOKE EVANS BALL is a wife, mother, freelance writer, and part-time librarian. She has been writing for more than twenty years after starting out as a newspaper reporter/feature writer/columnist in her hometown of Cleveland, Tennessee. She has had articles published in the *Cleveland Daily Banner, Farm Wife* magazine, *Moody Monthly* magazine, the *Charlotte Observer,* and the *Belmont Banner-Mount Holly News,* where she won awards for "Best People Story," "Best General Feature," and "Best Personal Column." She and her husband, Chris, reside in Charlotte, North Carolina, and are the parents of two grown children, Shane and Joanna. kisaword@bellsouth.net

COS BARNES is a former schoolteacher, newspaper columnist, and chamber of commerce public relations director. A freelance writer, she is the mother of three and the grandmother of six. She dances in a precision kickline of grandmothers whose ages range from fifty-six to seventy-five. She also plays handbells.

KAREN BERRY, OSF, lives in Tucson, Arizona, and has been a Franciscan Sister since 1962. Primarily a religious educator, she is also a writer, an Enneagram instructor, a Reiki practitioner, and a crafter. She has written many magazine articles, prayer pamphlets, and two books of Scripture reflections, *Beyond Broken Dreams* and *Signs Along Our Way*. Currently she is working on a book that links Enneagram personality types with the Gospel stories of healing. Her goal in life is to share the Franciscan values of joy, love for the Earth, and Gospel living. kberryosf@aol.com

DIANE GONZALES BERTRAND writes books for women of all ages. She is the author of *Close to the Heart, Lessons of the Game,* and *Sweet Fifteen,* all published by Arte Publico Press in Houston, Texas. It was during graduate school that her professors encouraged her to write stories and publish them. Because she didn't see enough books that featured Mexican-American characters, she wrote them herself. Her books have earned numerous awards, but her greatest accomplishments come in her daily roles as wife to Nick C. Bertrand and as mother to two teenagers, Nick and Suzanne. She teaches writing at St. Mary's University in San Antonio, Texas. Dbertrand@stmarytx.edu

ELIZABETH BEZANT was born in a small village in England and emigrated to Australia to marry and raise her young family. The continual flow of letters written by her, to the family she left behind, sparked a forgotten interest in writing. The basis for her positive, philosophical, fun, and sometimes unusual perspective on learning, living, and life comes from the eventful life that she and her husband lead, an outlook that comes through in her now internationally published work. elizabethbezant@iprimus.com.au

KAY BOLDEN was inspired as a child to become a writer after reading a poetry collection by Gwendolyn Brooks. While she still dabbles in poetry, personal essays are her first love. She and her children live in Joliet, where they share their backyard with a family of raccoons, a deaf squirrel, a stray frog, a pair of lost hummingbirds, and a pumpkin patch. k2bolden@aol.com

TERI BROWN is a freelance writer and homeschool author who lives, gardens, and homeschools her two children in Portland, Oregon.

RENIE SZILAK BURGHARDT, who was born in Hungary and came to the United States in 1951, is a freelance writer. Some of the publications in which her work has appeared are *Angels on Earth* magazine, *Mature Living, Fate, Cat Fancy, Midwest Living, Nostalgia,* and *The Friend.* She resides in Doniphan, Missouri. renieburghardt@semo .net

MARILYN BURKHARDT began her career as a city planner with the New York City Planning Commission. Writing is now her passion, and she particularly enjoys writing personal essays. Her essays have been published in several New York area newspapers and in some journals. She is now retired and enjoys a very active life taking advantage of the many cultural events and facilities in New York. She exercises daily and is particularly fond of swimming and other water-related activities. Ubram@aol.com

CHRISTINE M. CALDWELL resides in New Jersey with her husband and two daughters, Brooke and Jillian. She is a graduate of Rutgers-Camden and has recently completed her first novel. cmc013@gateway.net

TALIA CARNER is a novelist. Her novel, *Puppet Child,* was published in summer 2002. Her short stories appeared in *Rosebud, Midstream, Moxie,* and other literary reviews. Her personal essays appeared in *The New York Times, Lilith, Glory* (9/11) and *Happy*

Times Monthly among many others. Please check her website, www.TaliaCarner.com, or contact her at TaliaCarner@aol.com.

FERN CARNESS, MPH, RN, is a nurse health educator with a master's degree in public health who happens to be a breast cancer survivor. She is an international speaker who specializes in the areas of women's health, personal empowerment, and courage and survival. Known as the Voice for Women's Health, she is also a partner in Just Like a Woman, a specialty lingerie store for women with medical needs in Portland, Oregon. (503) 636-7513. Ferncarn@teleport.com

SUZANNE C. COLE taught English for many years at Houston Community College before retiring to write. She's authored college textbooks and *To Our Heart's Content: Meditations for Women Turning 50* as well as essays, poetry, plays, and short fiction. The anthologies *Gifts from Our Grandmothers, It's a Chick Thing, Grrrrr, Chicken Soup for the Traveler's Soul, Bless the Day, Get Well Wishes, Family Celebrations, Animal Blessings,* and *Mothers and Daughters* include her work. She is deeply grateful for the support of her family and a wonderful group of friends. An earlier version of this essay was published as "The End of a Marriage" in *Newsweek,* June 22, 1998. SuzAnneCC@aol.com

LISA A. CRAYTON is a freelance editor and writer with a dual B.S. degree with honors in public relations and journalism from Utica College of Syracuse University. Her career began in corporate communications. Today, she lives her dream of becoming a freelance writer. Her credits include features, profiles, columns, fillers, and essays. She has written for *Decision, Woman's Touch, Black Collegian, Next Step, Life@Work Journal, Charisma, eYOUth! Urban Family, Advanced Christian Writer,* and others. A committed Christian, gifted Bible teacher, and motivational speaker, she serves as a leader in her Maryland church where she delivers sermons and other motivational messages. dvscribe@worldnet.att.net

MARILYN D. DAVIS is a freelance writer living in the Chicago area. Her short stories and personal essays have been published in the local print media and at various websites. Her bachelor's and master's degrees are in education, and she has worked in both teaching and administrative capacities in educational settings ranging from preschool through college. She is married and the mother of two boys, ages ten and fourteen, who provide her with an endless source of material for her writings and who make her grateful every day for her sense of humor.

KAREN C. DRISCOLL lives in coastal Connecticut with her husband and four young children. While pregnant with twins she completed a master's degree in elementary and special education. Four years and four kids later she has embraced life as a stay-at-home mother. Looking for something creative to do while her children napped, she began recording her life with kids as a way of keeping in touch with friends and family. With naps now a distant memory, she continues to write and has been published in both books and magazines. kmhbrdriscoll@hotmail.com

CAROL F. FANTELLI was born in Cleveland, Ohio, and has lived in Raleigh, North Carolina, since 1974. She received her bachelor's degree in art from Meredith College in 1977 and began her career as a forensic facial reconstruction artist in 1982 working with various law enforcement agencies by reconstructing the faces of victims for identification purposes. She published her first forensic mystery in 1997, *The Face Finder,* and has completed a second forensic mystery in a new series, which is not yet published, and is currently working on a third. Her books are based loosely on her twenty years' experience as a forensic sculptor and are works of fiction. www.grapevine-pub.com. Facefinders@aol.com

DEBBIE FARMER writes the award-winning syndicated column *Family Daze.* Her essays have appeared in *Reader's Digest, Family*

Fun Magazine, The Christian Science Monitor, various books in the *Chicken Soup* series, and hundreds of newspapers and parenting magazines in the United States, Canada, and Australia. She's the author of the book *Life in the Fast Food Lane: Surviving the Chaos of Parenting.* For more information about her column, visit: www.familydaze.com, or features@familydaze.com

SUSAN FARR-FAHNCKE is a freelance writer living in Utah. She writes for inspirational books and magazines and runs a website and daily list of inspirational stories. She has recently published her book, *Angel's Legacy,* a tribute to her inspiring sister who lost her battle with a brain tumor. Susan@2theheart.com. www.2THEHEART.com

CAROL FEWELL is a writer who recently relocated from California to a small town near Salem, Oregon, where she lives with her husband. cairynskye@yahoo.com

JUDITH MORTON FRASER, MFT, a psychotherapist in Los Angeles, is also a writer and actress. Her short stories have been published in the *L.A. Times, Everywoman's Village, Hallmark, Chocolate for a Woman's Heart,* and *Chocolate for a Woman's Spirit,* and articles dealing with relationships and addictions have appeared in the California Association of Marriage & Family Therapists' newsletters. She is currently writing a novel combining creativity, Native American ceremonies, and life passages. She and her husband, Ian, an eleven-time Emmy Award winner, have two grown children, a son and daughter, and three grandchildren. (323) 656-9800. phrasmusu@earthlink.net

JOANNE M. FRIEDMAN was born and raised in New Jersey. She has a BA in psychology from Clark University, Worcester, Massachusetts, and a MEd in special education from the University of Hartford. She has been a teacher and a writer for thirty years and is currently teaching high-school English. She lives with her daughter and her partner in Sussex County, New Jersey, on the horse farm she owns and operates. She writes a humor column on the subject of horses that appears in several local newspapers in Massachusetts. jmfriedman@nac.net

BEVERLY FROEHLICH continues to write—both poetry and a book of creative nonfiction concerning the lives of her great-grandparents—while residing in a small, turn-of-the-century farmhouse in Beavercreek, Oregon. Poems written while she circled the country riding along in her husband's eighteen-wheeler have been recently published in *synesthesia* and the self-published *Lost Photographs*. Her poem "Lucky You" appeared in the spring 2002 issue of *Clackamas Literary Review.* (503) 632-5449

LUCI N. FULLER is an essayist whose work has appeared in magazines and books around the country. She is also the author of the nonfiction book titled *Where the Universe Breathes: Lessons from a Sacred Journey,* which her agent is now circulating. She lives in the scenic Pacific Northwest, and welcomes writing assignments and other correspondence. (503) 492-4317. LuciFuller@aol.com

JEAN JEFFREY GIETZEN is author of the Christian Gift Book best-seller *If You're Missing Baby Jesus,* published by Multnomah. Her stories have also been published in *Chocolate for a Teen's Soul,* *A Second Chicken Soup for the Woman's Soul,* and *Chicken Soup for the Gardener's Soul.* A wife, mother, and grandmother, she lives in Tucson, Arizona, and Milwaukee, Wisconsin. She leads writing workshops in both states. (520) 296-1550 or (414) 352-2009. Octodon31469@cs.com

DAWN GOLDSMITH is a multipublished writer of nonfiction, short stories, and essays and also reviews books for *Publishers Weekly* and Crescent Blues E'Magazine. www.crescentblues.com

HEATHER GOLDSMITH lives in Western Australia with her husband and two children. She's a wife and mother who also enjoys reading, writing, and anything to do with the written word. Currently working on her first novel, she also writes nonfiction and short stories. Having some work published in Australian magazines and in various places online has encouraged her to pursue her dream of becoming a successful published author. bwheather@hotmail.com

ANNE GOODRICH is the proud mother of three wonderfully unique individuals: Gordon, Kelly, and Carman. She is employed as a graphic and web designer in Kalamazoo, Michigan, and greatly enjoys nibbling a bonbon while trying her hand at short story writing. In addition, she devotes herself to working on OhAngel!com, her inspirational ecard website, at http://www.ohangel.com.

JODY GREENLEE, a pediatric nurse, is the patient care coordinator for Children of the Americas, a nonprofit organization that arranges stateside medical care for children of Guatemala. Her volunteer work with this organization recently led to a medical mission trip to Guatemala. She and her family hosted Edson, a medically fragile foster child with C.O.T.A. As a firm believer in the power of the human connection, she believes in sharing her God-given talents and fortune with others. Her passions include her husband, Tom, and their three children. Freelance writing allows her to provide a written voice for those not able to tell their own stories. Green71957@aol.com

JUDY GRUEN is the author of *Carpool Tunnel Syndrome: Motherhood as Shuttle Diplomacy* and *Till We Eat Again: Confessions of a Diet Dropout* (Champion Press). To receive her free semimonthly humor column, sign up at www.championpress.com/offmy noodle/htm. judy@championpress.com

WENDY STOFAN HALLEY has had a dream to inspire others to awaken to their true and powerful selves through her work as a counselor, lecturer, and writer. She and her husband, John, combined their skills to create Lucid Path Healing Arts as a way to realize this dream. She also wrote *Inside Out*—a children's story whose message inspires readers of all ages to remember who they really are—which will be published by Illumination Arts in spring 2003. www.lucidpath.com

JULIE HARTMANS has an English degree and has taught English as a second language. At present, she is building a massage therapy clientele. She considers herself a bit of a nomad, having lived in numerous states. She is a single mom of a one-year-old son and currently lives in the Twin Cities area of Minnesota. Reading and writing have been focal points in her life, plus a keen interest in all things metaphysical. She has articles posted on several Internet sites, including FitnessHeaven.com. A member of the Society of Children's Book Writers and Illustrators, she is working on a middle-grade novel. juliehartmans@attbi.com

MARCIE HENDERSON is an aspiring writer who was born and raised in northeastern Pennsylvania. She lives there today with the love of her life, husband Jay, and their green iguana named Stanley. She has worked eleven-plus years in the manufacturing industry. She has had many assignments ranging from operating a diaper production line to administrative and technical support in computer systems. She enjoys writing poetry and personalized cards for all occasions. She hopes to someday publish a romance novel and currently has three in the works. Her hobbies include sewing, ceramics, bowling, and occasionally singing karaoke. mah_ink@hotmail.com

SHEILA S. HUDSON, Bright Ideas founder, freelance writer, and speaker, wife/mother/grandmother, is published in *Chocolate for a Teen's Heart, Chocolate for a Teen's Soul, The Expressive Heart, Chocolate for a Woman's Blessing, Chocolate for a Woman's Heart, God's Vitamin C for the Spirit of Men, Taking Education Higher, Casas por Cristo: Stories from the Border, Chocolate for a Woman's Dreams,* and *Life's Little Rule Book.* She is a columnist for *Christian Standard* and frequent contributor to *Lookout* and *Athens Magazine.* (706) 546-5085. Fax: (706) 546-7419. sheila-brightideas@home.com; www.sheila-brightideas.com

CINDY KAUFFMAN is a weekly humorist in Green, Ohio, where she lives with her husband and four children. She has written more than two hundred printed columns and was previously published in *Chocolate for a Woman's Dreams.* CinKau75@aol.com

ELIZABETH KRENIK (TRAXLER) is a mother of three daughters and a first-grade teacher. She enjoys spending time with her family and friends and keeps busy with gardening, reading, traveling, and performing a reader's theater presentation that she wrote about her brother's fight against AIDS. ektrax@frontiernet.net

BONITA (BONNIE) LAETTNER was an elementary teacher for twenty-eight years. She has a master's degree in education. She is on the Newsletter Committee of the Mothers of Professional Basketball Players. She has written two books about her family that she hopes to have published.

KATHRYN LAY lives in Texas with her daughter and husband. She homeschools and writes full-time. Her writing has appeared in *Guideposts, Woman's Day, Chocolate for a Woman's Blessings,* and many others. rlay15@aol.com

WENDY (REID CRISP) LESTINA is a public speaker and the author of two books, *100 Things I'm Not Going to Do Now That I'm Over 50* and *Do As I Say, Not As I Did: Perfect Advice from an Imperfect Mother,* both from Penguin/Putnam/Perigee. She was formerly a magazine editor (*Savvy*) and the national director of the National Association for Female Executives. She has an honorary Doctor of Letters degree from Middlebury College, Middlebury, Vermont. She lives on a farm in northern California with her husband, John. annabel144@yahoo.com

BEVERLY C. LUCEY has published fiction in *Portland Maine Magazine, Flint River Review,* and *Moxie,* and four of her stories appear in *We Teach Them All* (Stenhouse Press). She edits two ezines: www.languagewrangler.com for educators and word lovers and www.womanofacertainage.com. She can also be seen in ezines: TW3 ezine, Zoetrope All-Story Extra—Gift Wrap, and in Vestal Review—Waiting for the Flight. She is an instructor of education at Agnes Scott College.

CHRIS MIKALSON lives with her husband in Alberta, Canada, and has two daughters and three grandchildren, two girls and a boy. She works full-time as a bookkeeper for a car dealership. On weekends and evenings, when not spending time with the grandkids, she pursues her love of writing. She has had articles published in *Grandparents Today* and *Woman's World* and writes for the "Soapbox" of her local newspaper. Her biggest project, a romance novel, is waiting for its second draft. i-mik@telusplanet.net

CAROL SJOSTROM MILLER lives in New Jersey with her husband, Jack, and daughter, Stephanie. Looking for something quiet to do during her daughter's naps, she started writing and hasn't looked back. Her articles and essays have been published in a variety of national and regional magazines, and she is currently pursuing her master's degree in English and publishing at Rosemont College. miller_carol@usa.net

PAULA CONRAD MLEKUSH began writing after going back to college when her only child left the nest. She thanks her college professors for encouraging her to submit her work for publication. A proud member of Phi Beta Kappa, she continues to write stories and essays. She divides her time between her home in Greensboro, North Carolina, and a Blue Ridge Mountain retreat. When not writing, she loves reading, working in her flower garden, spending time with friends, family, and her beloved cocker spaniel, and sipping that perfect glass of chardonnay with her chocolate. pmlekush@triad.rr.com

DIANE NOVINSKI is a widowed mother of two who has written several inspirational stories after experiencing the sadness and pain of losing her husband, Ben, to cancer. She is dedicated to raising two happy, healthy children, who have emerged whole and sound from the tragedy of the death of a parent during their childhood. With the knowledge that no person who has deeply touched one's life can ever be taken away, she hopes her story will bring comfort, strength, and hope to someone going through difficult times. She has also published in the *Chicken Soup* series. She lives in Old Saybrook, Connecticut, with her children, Jared and Lara. dianenovinski@hotmail.com

CINDI PEARCE has a bachelor's degree in journalism from Ohio University, and for years has worked as a newspaper reporter/columnist/editor and photographer. She is a freelance writer, and her fiction has appeared nine times in *Star* magazine and has also appeared in *True Love, True Romance,* and *True Experience* magazines. She has worked as a contract writer for a teen pregnancy prevention project and Family and Children First Council. She has also worked as a court advocate for a domestic violence agency, a choreographer, tap dancing teacher, yoga instructor, and divorce investigator. She is studying to become a certified graphologist (handwriting analyst). She is married and the mother of three teenagers.

MICHELLE PEARSON is a freelance writer whose work has appeared in *Obadiah Magazine, Becoming Family, Chicago Parent, God Allows U-Turns,* and numerous other print and online publications. Her syndicated weekly column on the ups and downs of family life is celebrating its fourth year in existence. When not writing, she works as an education assistant at the Byron Forest Preserve in Byron, Illinois, teaching children about nature and the environment. She has three grown daughters and lives with her husband, Jeff, and son Sean on a fifth-generation family farm in northern Illinois. stoneyknoll@lrnetl.com

LAVERNE BARDY POLLAK is a freelance humor writer. Her column, *Laverne's View,* appears in two New Jersey newspapers. In addition, she works as a features writer, journalist, and copywriter for various other publications. She is currently working on three books: a memoir, a book of essays, and a children's book. She is co-originator of the Working Writer's Roundtable, an organization composed of serious writers working at their craft. The Roundtable, which is under the auspices of the Sussex County Arts & Heritage Council in Newton, New Jersey, solicits authors, publishers, agents, editors, photographers, and others to speak informally to the group. (973) 383-1088. Lavernep@ erols.com

LOIS ERISEY POOLE is the author of a book, *Ring Around the Moon.* She has been syndicated throughout the country and has had freelance articles published in many national publications. She writes a weekly column in *The Antelope Press* and is a popular speaker in the Southern California region. She teaches classes that instruct students on how to write about the significant moments of their lives.

CINDY POTTER and her husband, Dan, share their lives with their three dogs, Windy Rose, Ozzie, and Kimo, and cats Peanut, Magic, and Itty Bitty. During their twenty-eight-year marriage, they have rescued and then found the homes of or found new homes for over two hundred stray animals. ljpotter@attbi.com

FELICE R. PRAGER is a freelance writer from Scottsdale, Arizona. Her work has appeared in international, national, and local publications, as well as many ezines. FelPrager@aol.com. http://www.writefunny.com

SALLIE A. RODMAN is a freelance writer residing in Los Alamitos, California, with her husband of thirty-six years, a cat, and a dog. She has three grown children, a son and two daughters, and two grandchildren. She holds a certificate in Bach Flower Therapy and Reiki II. She also works in the corporate world as an administrative support manager. She enjoys writing about the synchronicity of life and universal themes in everyday events. Her hobbies include gardening, collecting first editions, and studying holistic avenues of health. She is currently working on a book of her experience with panic attack syndrome and agoraphobia. (562) 596-7917. srodman@ix.netcom.com

MAUREEN MARY ROSENBERG is a freelance writer living in the foothills of northern California with her black Lab, Bucky, and her husband, Jay, whom she credits with "ruffling the feathers of her soul" while giving her unbridled encouragement to follow her bliss. She is a graduate of Writer's Digest School, poet, and short story writer, and is currently working on her first novel. prairierose@volcano.net

LISA SANDERS is a stay-home mom to two preschoolers, Torri and Teague. She says her husband, Rich, is her best friend, boyfriend, and one true love. Although she no longer stands in front of a classroom, this former teacher believes she has "chalk dust on the sleeve of her soul." A nationally published freelance writer, she specializes in family and education articles. Samples of her work can be viewed at her website: www.Joy-Writer.com. Lisa@ Joy-Writer.com

HARRIET MAY SAVITZ is an author and essayist who brings inspirational-based fiction and nonfiction to her readers. Her books (more than twenty-one to date) help both young adolescents and adults rediscover life with all its possibilities. Her latest book, *Messages from Somewhere* (Little Treasure Publications), will be released in 2002. An earlier book, *Growing Up at 62,* is also published by Little Treasure Publications. One of her books, *Run, Don't Walk* (YA—reissued), was adapted as an ABC Afterschool Special produced by Henry Winkler. hmaysavitz@aol.com. www.harrietmaysavitz.com

DEANNA DOSS SHRODES is a minister who has served with her pastor-husband, Larry, in churches for the last fifteen years. She is a pianist, singer, composer, recording artist, choral director, and freelance writer. In addition to pastoral ministry, she enjoys a wide range of speaking engagements at many church services, revivals, retreats, conferences, camps, and community events, with her forte being ministry to women. Bringing a message that life circumstances are not meant to break but to shape individuals is her life's passion. She and her husband have three children, Dustin, Jordan, and Savanna Rose. Her website ministry is devoted to women pastors and pastors' wives who are "highly involved" in church ministry: www.pastoringpartners.com. PastorDeanna@aol.com

SHELLEY SIGMAN is a freelance writer and photographer who, after twenty-one years heading her own landscape design company, traded her T-square for the tools of writing. She is an entertainment reporter for the *Main Line Times* in suburban Philadelphia and former lifestyle feature writer and restaurant columnist for Gannett Newspapers. She's had articles, humor, and fiction featured in *The Chicago Tribune, Philadelphia's Exponent, Green's Magazine,* and *Reader's Break.* siggie@enter.net

BETH M. SKARUPA was born in Chicago, lived in São Paulo, Brazil, as a preteen, then moved to Alabama when she was in high school. She has a BA in communication arts from the University of Alabama at Huntsville and an MA in critical studies of film/television from the University of California, Los Angeles. She has been a reporter for an army newspaper for the past three years and currently works as a freelance writer and full-time mom. She lives in Alabama with her husband, Andrew, and their three young children, Alexis, Elena, and Nicholas.

JUDITH SLOAN is a speaker, book reviewer, and freelance writer whose articles have appeared in *The New York Times, Newsday, Archives of Internal Medicine,* and *Children's Hospital Quarterly.* She also sings with the Juilliard Choral Union. A former English teacher at New Rochelle High School, she was senior writer at Long Island Jewish Medical Center. She received her BA degree from Brandeis University and a MAT degree from Harvard University. Judith and husband Mort live in Sands Point, New York. jsloan@optonline.net

SHEILA STEPHENS is an international award-winning poet, writing teacher, columnist, and speaker who enjoys helping people build their lives "from the inside, out." To her, self-esteem is a spiritual journey of accepting the seed of love that divine spirit places in each heart. She has just completed *Walking with the Flowers: 50 Weeks of Quiet Meditations for a Woman's Busy World.* Her professional services include creativity coaching, personalized correspondence writing classes (available worldwide), and "Walking with the Flowers" seminars.

DONNA STONE is a freelance writer and stay-at-home mom. She writes articles and essays on various topics, including parenting, health, family, and environmental issues. She is currently working on journalizing the difficulties of coping with multiple chemical sensitivities in our modern world. donna_stone_m@yahoo.com

FRANCINE M. STOREY is a poet and playwright and her production, *The Hour of Lead at the Ensemble Theatre*, was accepted into The Samuel French Short Play Festival, 2000. Other plays have been produced off-off Broadway by the Women's Ensemble, the Abingdon, the Impact, and the Vox Theatre companies. A collection of poems, *Dead in the Snows of Love*, was filmed by the Vox. Her poem "Instructions for Search," winner of the Dylan Thomas Poetry Prize from the New School in New York City, is featured in the film *A Fish Out of Time*, Third Wave Media Productions. Publications include *The Journal of Irish Literature*, *The Art and Craft of Poetry*, and *By Actors, For Actors*, Volumes I, II, and III. She has been accepted into The Pen and Brush, one of the oldest women's art organizations in the United States.

JULIE TEASDALE is currently a domestic engineer at her home in Bakersfield, California, with her biggest projects being daughter Abby, son Adam, and hubby David. In her "previous life" she was an elementary-school teacher. Now, when the children sleep, she enjoys writing, reading, animals, and managing the All Better Club, a charity that was founded in Abby's honor to help hospitalized children and their families. If you would like to know more about their organization, visit their website at http://members.spree.com/family/allbetter or e-mail allbetter club@aol.com.

NANCY TOMAZIC is the published author of several short stories. She is currently working on her first novel. writinfool@sim con.net

GERALDINE (GERRY) TRICKLE balances write-for-business projects with creating fiction and nonfiction. She is a published author of personal essays. Her writing voice speaks with the wisdom gained from navigating the rocky shoals of Love and Loss, surviving the Straits of Single Parenting, and sailing in Relationship Regatas. Today, she frequently drops anchor in GrandChildren Bay then heads back to New Jersey to tend to a novel-in-progress. www.writeronline.com or gtworks@home.com

PEGGY VINCENT is a retired midwife who has welcomed more than twenty-five hundred babies into the world. She lives in Oakland, California, with Roger, her husband of thirty-six years, and Skylar, their teenage son. Two adult children, Colin and Jill, live nearby. Her first book, *Baby Catcher: Chronicles of a Modern Midwife,* was released by Scribner in spring 2002. In addition to working on a sequel, she writes fiction and short essays. Visit her website at www.babycatcher.net and sign the guest book or send her an e-mail: PV@peggyvincent.com.

LINDA H. WATERMAN is a successful freelance proofreader who finally decided to do some writing of her own. Born in Connecticut, she has traveled the world and spent a life-changing year living in Rome, Italy. Today she resides in California, where she tries to perpetuate a Mediterranean lifestyle—while writing what she hopes are amusing essays. LINDAWAT@aol.com

ANNE CULBREATH WATKINS resides in Alabama and her writing has appeared in publications such as *American Caged-Bird Magazine, Angels on Earth, Bird Talk,* and *Writer's Digest Forum.* A regular contributor to the Guideposts hardcover book series *Listening to the Animals,* she has more stories scheduled to appear in the Guideposts book *Their Mysterious Ways.* She is the author of *A New Owner's Guide to Conures,* T.F.H. Publications. http://www.geocities.com/anne_c_watkins

LISA WEST is a freelance writer, computer geek, political junkie, and softball fanatic. She is the West Coast editor and editorial columnist for The Einkwell (www.einkwell.com), an online magazine. She lives in Portland, Oregon, with her two daughters. thatgirl@pacifier.com

KRISTINE ZIEMNIK is a native Ohioan, a wife, and a mother of four. She lives at Chippewa Lake and enjoys boating and swimming. She has a poet's heart and has won a poetry contest with "America Is Still the Best Place to Be" and has had one poem turned into a song titled "The Bethlehem Story." A floral designer by profession, she's also been a crafter all her life. She started her own business in 1997, called Kristine's Kreations, and markets a gift item called "Bottles of Tears" quite successfully to Christian bookstores. She was first published nationally in *Angels on Earth* magazine and hopes that "A Christmas Surprise" will remind people what is truly important in life. She hopes to write a book someday. (330) 769-2931. Zemies4mom@aol.com

ACKNOWLEDGMENTS

My untold gratitude goes to the contributors of this book. Their sweet bravery is contagious. The magnificent richness of their stories will be felt by women throughout the world.

Continued thanks go to my agent, Peter Miller, and his staff, and my editor, Caroline Sutton, and the Fireside / Simon & Schuster team for their remarkable faith in the *Chocolate* series.

My gratitude and deep love to my husband, Eric, who demonstrates courage with every creative turn he takes. And, as always, I send my unconditional love for my family and friends.

I'm reminded of how grateful I am that God spoke to me before the *Chocolate* series began. He said, "Write a book for women; you're a woman of courage." How appropriate, then, that there is this sequel.

ABOUT THE AUTHOR

Kay Allenbaugh is the author of *Chocolate for a Woman's Soul; Chocolate for a Woman's Heart; Chocolate for a Woman's Heart and Soul; Chocolate for a Lover's Heart; Chocolate for a Mother's Heart; Chocolate for a Woman's Spirit; Chocolate for a Teen's Soul; Chocolate for a Woman's Blessings; Chocolate for a Teen's Heart; Chocolate for a Woman's Dreams;* and *Chocolate for a Teen's Spirit.* She resides in Lake Oswego, Oregon, with her husband, Eric Allenbaugh, author of *Deliberate Success: Realize Your Vision with Purpose, Passion and Performance* and *Wake-Up Calls: You Don't Have to Sleepwalk Through Your Life, Love or Career!*